Witnessing

Witnessing

Prophecy, Politics, and Wisdom

Edited by
Maria Clara Bingemer and Peter Casarella

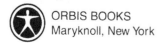

ORBIS BOOKS
Maryknoll, New York

ORBIS BOOKS
Maryknoll, New York 10545

Fathers and Brothers
MARYKNOLL™

Founded in 1970, Orbis Books endeavors to publish works that enlighten the mind, nourish the spirit, and challenge the conscience. The publishing arm of the Maryknoll Fathers and Brothers, Orbis seeks to explore the global dimensions of the Christian faith and mission, to invite dialogue with diverse cultures and religious traditions, and to serve the cause of reconciliation and peace. The books published reflect the views of their authors and do not represent the official position of the Maryknoll Society. To learn more about Maryknoll and Orbis Books, please visit our website at www.maryknollsociety.org.

Library of Congress Cataloging-in-Publication Data

Witnessing : prophecy, politics, and wisdom / Maria Clara Bingemer and
    Peter Casarella, editors
        pages   cm
Includes bibliographical references and index.
ISBN 978-1-62698-087-7 (pbk.)
1. Witness bearing (Christianity). 2. Martyrdom—Christianity—History—
20th century. I. Bingemer, Maria Clara Lucchetti, editor of compilation.
    BV4520.W546   2014
    248'.5—dc23

                                                    2014012451

Contents

Preface

Maria Clara Bingemer
and Peter Casarella

Witnessing is a term that can be confusing. It can be mistaken for proselytism. In addition, its translation into other languages (*martyresthai, testimonio, testemunha,* etc.) yields a semantic field richer and more varied than the legalistic overtones of the English word. In its biblical context it can carry a juridical meaning, but the mindset of the courtroom does not exhaust its meaning. To others it might seem like a rhetorical flourish, but the recognition of an act of witnessing creates much more than emotional attachment to the memory and message of the witness.

Witnessing illuminates a path that can be followed. One stands in the company of the poor of Jesus Christ, and their example of sanctity and justice marks out the direction of the journey. The texts that record the act and the words and deeds archived into memory come back to life when the follower recognizes that these fixed deposits of experience suggest both crisis and renewal in one's own way of life. Christians calls this path discipleship and enter it wholeheartedly in spite of the known cost.

Such is the case with the celebration of the twenty-third anniversary of the martyrs of the Universidad Centroamericana (UCA) that took place at DePaul University in Chicago in November 2012. The tragic loss of innocent life was mourned, and the gifts of the Jesuits and their companions were recalled. We join ourselves to the very words of Jon Sobrino, S.J., who in November 1989, after finding out the horrible news of what transpired in his absence, flew from Thailand to Santa Clara and jotted down this prayer: "May they rest in peace, Ignacio Ellacuría, Ignacio Martín-Baró, Segundo Montes,

Joaquín López y López, Juan Moreno, and Armando López; may they rest in peace, brothers and fellow journeyers with Jesus; may Celina and Elba Ramos also rest in peace, daughters truly loved by God. May they rest in peace; may they never allow us to rest in peace."[1]

But our focus was not just praise and blame. It included reflection on the challenge of offering and receiving a witness. Consider an illustrative example cited at the opening of the event. We recalled to a large and engaged crowd a local testimony, one largely forgotten but hardly removed in space or time from our meeting place in Chicago's busy Loop. Outside of Calvert House, the Catholic Chaplaincy of the University of Chicago in the Hyde Park neighborhood of Chicago, lies a bronze plaque with a visage. This record memorializes Fr. Ignacio Martín-Baró, S.J., "Nacho," as he was once known by his peers in the program in social psychology at the university. Do the students and faculty who participate in the daily Mass know the full significance of that plaque, a memorial designed by a priest from Chicago? In other words, one of the Jesuit martyrs completed a Master's and Ph.D. program in Chicago in the late 1970s before returning to El Salvador. Nacho had a love–hate relationship with the United States but dove into academic and pastoral life in that setting, submitted himself to its rigor and intensity, and took that training back to his native land.[2] He produced scholarship with great vigor for ten years to the day after the approval of his dissertation. What legacy, besides a bronze plaque, is left behind for us? That question was not specifically addressed, but it merits mention precisely because it forces us to think about the challenge presented not just by the Jesuit martyrs but by all Christian witnessing.

The Jesuit martyrs and their companions fit into the pattern of the Bible and the early church.[3] As Jon Sobrino suggests, in life and death they witnessed to the coming of the kingdom in accord with Jesus' Sermon on the Plain:

---

1. As cited in the chapter by Jon Sobrino in this volume.

2. Nelson Portillo, "The Life of Ignacio Martín-Baró: A Narrative Account of a Personal Biographical Journey," *Peace and Conflict: Journal of Peace Psychology* 18 (2012): 77-87, here at 80-81.

3. See Peter Casarella, "Conversion and Witnessing: Intercultural Renewal in a World Church," *Catholic Theological Society of America Proceedings* 68 (2013): 4-7, and the literature cited therein.

Blessed are you who are poor, for the kingdom of God is yours.
Blessed are you who are now hungry, for you will be satisfied.
Blessed are you who are now weeping, for you will laugh.
Blessed are you when people hate you, and when they exclude
   and insult you, and denounce your name as evil on account
   of the Son of Man. (Luke 6:20-23)

Like Archbishop Romero, prophetic witnesses see the Suffering Servant of Second Isaiah in the crucified people whom they accompany: "Even as many were amazed at him—so marred were his features, beyond that of mortals his appearance, beyond that of human beings" (Isaiah 52:14). The disfigurement of the poor is palpable in their condition of suffering. The plight of the people on the margins is furthermore personified by the prophet's realistic image of redemption through innocent suffering: "He was spurned and avoided by men, a man of suffering, knowing pain, like one from whom you turn your face, spurned, and we held him in no esteem" (Isaiah 53:3).

Witnessing opens up new horizons for theological reflection. This volume explores many new horizons seen from different perspectives within global Catholicism: U.S. Latino/a Catholicism, the church of the poor in Brazil, U.S. political theology, postcolonial theology in Manila, Latin American liberation theology, and black theology, to name just a few. What themes emerge? We cite here just a few examples, knowing that many more are elaborated by the individual authors.

First, in the words of Archbishop Oscar Romero, "God speaks from within history."[4] We still face the threat today of a disincarnate faith, a self-enclosed attitude that treats religious beliefs like commodities that exist solely for the benefit of a private self. The most serious reply to the new dualisms is the presentation in narrative form of the flesh and blood of the witnesses we have considered. Witnessing is a vital form of pedagogy in our times. "Modern [woman or] man listens more willingly to witnesses than to teachers, and if [she

---

4. Maria Clara Luchetti Bingemer, "La fe: Otra mirada para leer la historia. Monseñor Romero: Una clave de lectura testimonial," *Revista latinoamericana de teología* 80 (2010): 175-93, here at 191, citing Romero's homily from February 18, 1979.

or] he does listen to teachers, it is because they are witnesses."[5] The flesh and blood of the witnesses lead us to the flesh and blood of the Scriptures with new insights and perspectives:

> Here is an important path for Christian faith in the contemporary world: to recuperate the story of God that generates faith. In addition, and no less significantly, to recuperate the story of the witnesses, witnesses who weave this history out of their experience, their commitment, their testimony, and their blood. And this can be disclosed if faith is treated as an event, as an experience revealed in the middle of history. Faith is a glance, a way of gazing at reality (*una mirada*), a perspective from which one can read and interpret this history. Faith is the interpretive key that permits us to comprehend history under God's gaze.[6]

Witnessing focusses the gaze of faith firmly on the reality in front of us while still allowing God's gaze on that reality to empower our engagement with God and with our own history in the making.

Second, biography and personal memory can play a key role in theology.[7] Lay witnesses like the inimitable Simone Weil, our late modern Sybil, teach us that mysticism and spiritual interiority are not meant for promoting social isolation. As creatures made of flesh and bone we narrate our existence almost as a biological instinct. But these personal testimonies need not take introspection as the last word. Christian witnessing reminds us that the memorializing born of solitude is a path to rediscovering the biography of Jesus. His life is the prototypical confessional literature of the mystical life.[8] In that light we are led outward, to the margins. Jesus leads us to rewrite our biographies in the company of the poor. We live in the hope that the text with which we end our lives is marked by such a transformation. In this sense, the theologian today can approach the genre of

---

5. Pope Paul VI, address to the members of the *Consilium de Laicis* (October 2, 1974), in *Acta Apostolica Sedis* 66 (1974): 568. See also *Evangelii nuntiandi* #41.

6. Bingemer, "La fe," 180.

7. Maria Clara Bingemer, *O mistério e o mundo: Paixão por Deus em tempos de descrença* (Rio de Janeiro: Rocco, 2013), 351-58. This book is scheduled to be published by Cascade Press in 2015 as *The Mystery and the World: Passion for God in Times of Disbelief*.

8. Ibid., 355.

biography and re-examine the speculative foundations of his or her own method.

Third, Christian spirituality is a testimony to God's beauty. At first this sounds like a merely poetic utterance, a flight from the grim realities of lived social inequality to an idealized romantic haven. But the essays in this volume show how beauty and justice interpenetrate and beckon simultaneously for the consideration of the faithful, including of course the faithful theologian. The exemplar here is the *Magnificat* of Mary (Luke 1:46-55). Singing praise to the grandeur of God and rejoicing in the Lord are acts of personal testimony. It arises from the heart that has been entrusted to the Lord. But it does not encourage passive subservience except to doing the will of the Lord in faith and in history. Mary famously proclaims:

> He has shown might with his arm,
>   dispersed the arrogant of mind and heart.
> He has thrown down the rulers from their thrones
>   but lifted up the lowly.
> The hungry he has filled with good things;
>   the rich he has sent away empty. (Luke 1:51-53)

This prophetic and sometimes discordant witness is nonetheless in complete harmony with Mary's song of praise for the beauty of divine mercy. Betrothed to God's beauty, she sings in solidarity with God's poor.

Fourth, witnessing can and should be linked to intercultural dialogue. With this volume, we are sharing acts of witnessing as an invitation to dialogue. "To (have a) dialogue means to believe that the 'other' has something worthwhile to say, and to entertain his or her point of view and perspective," Pope Francis wrote in his first address on social communications.[9] "Engaging in dialogue does not mean renouncing our own ideas and traditions, but the pretense that they alone are valid and absolute." The contributions in this volume were the results of a meeting in Chicago of women and men who are exercising leadership in the church in Asia, Latin America, and North America. The conversations we began were intended to model the

---

9. Pope Francis, Message for the Forty-Eighth World Day of Social Communications, January 23, 2014.

church of the future, an exchange of gifts in which the North and the South learn from each other.

Prophecy, politics, and wisdom are not three separate forms of witnessing. The chapters of this book speak eloquently to the necessity of each as well as to their unity. To borrow a phrase from Gustavo Gutiérrez, the words and deeds of the witnesses "x-ray" us.[10] The praxis of the Word of God in the life of a witness is "living and active, sharper than any two-edged sword" (Hebrews 4:12). We did not put this book together to place the Jesuit martyrs on a pedestal. As Michael Budde argues, we attend also to the counterwitness of our own actions and those of the church and the ways in which we fail to live up to beauty and goodness of the Lord's own witness.

The production of this volume bears witness to a fruitful relationship with a wealth of able collaborators. Many of these testimonies would remain silent if we did not acknowledge them here. First of all, we would like to thank DePaul University and the remarkable staff at the Center for World Catholicism and Intercultural Theology. The support of William T. Cavanaugh, Francis Salinel, and Karen Kraft was essential in organizing the conference in Chicago. Second, we were blessed with the generous and able assistance of two research assistants at the University of Notre Dame, Andrew Geist and Jonathan Wilcoxson. Finally, we thank our editor at Orbis Books, Robert Ellsberg, for his patient encouragement and unmatched expertise.

Finally, we offer these words with much gratitude for the always-inspiring testimony of João Batista Libanio, S.J. (1932-2014). He went to the Lord on January 30, 2014, as we were putting the finishing touches on this manuscript. His witness as a friend, collaborator, and as a Jesuit scholar of immense erudition surpasses the pivotal role he played in inaugurating the first generation of theologians of liberation in Brazil. *Descanse na paz do Senhor Jesus.*

---

10. Gustavo Gutiérrez, *On Job: God-Talk and the Suffering of the Innocent* (Maryknoll, NY: Orbis Books, 1987), xvii.

1

Testimony: Mysticism with Open Eyes

Maria Clara Lucchetti Bingemer

A witness, in legal terms, is a person who has seen and/or heard something important and is able to provide information and details about it. A witness is, therefore, someone who tells of some lived experience, now recorded in memory. The testimony is, then, the public assertion by the person who has seen, heard, experienced, and remembered what happened, which is then collected by others who have authority to ensure its validity. It could be conceived as a subjective experience opened to public access in order to establish justice and restore broken order, or perhaps even to indicate those who were affected by some harm or who may benefit from the telling of the narrative.

The word *testimony* is crucial to the history of Christianity. Faith in Jesus Christ, in whom the community recognizes the Word made flesh, revealing the merciful Father, was communicated through time by narratives and texts that attested to his existence, his words and actions. But before that, these witnesses transmitted their faith orally. People who were true "living texts," in whose flesh the Holy Spirit had written—not with ink, but with its own divine breath—were the foundations of the new law of love. Paul of Tarsus says to the Christians of Corinth that they are "a letter from Christ, entrusted to our care, written not with ink but with the Spirit of the living God; not on stone tablets but on the tablets of human hearts" (2 Corinthians 3:3, ESV).

Quite often, this faith was transmitted through written texts by witnesses who bore them sealed in the fragility of their hearts of flesh. A few of them, at the outset, were eyewitnesses who saw and believed in the deeds and sayings of Jesus of Nazareth. They started calling him

"Lord" and "Christ." Distant from those historical facts, in the twenty-first century many of us are now hearing witnesses who have believed the announcement of the good news of the gospel narrated through the church. Even so, we are witnesses who have lived the experience of the strong presence of the Risen Christ within ourselves and therefore cannot remain silent but are driven to communicate what we believe to others.[1]

In the midst of secularization, through the insecure paths of postmodernity, historic Christianity is experiencing a profound crisis of its institutions, rules, and official dogmatic formulations. It is a time when we, people of faith, are called to be "awaken[ed] from dogmatic slumber, from which Kant wanted to liberate us."[2] In addition, this awakening helps us to realize that there are two ways of doing theology: one setting out from the texts of Scripture and tradition and the other setting out from witnesses who tell the story of their experience of God, converting into flesh the concepts and categories that theoretical texts produce and interpret. Both are in a permanent hermeneutic circle. However, today, perhaps more than ever, the theology that emerges from the narrative testimony is more readily heard due to the fact of its charism for interruptive interpellation. Narrative testimony challenges those who are struggling between the crisis of modernity and the Enlightenment, or between reason and *liquefaction*, that is, postmodernity.[3]

Doing theology beginning from the narratives of witnesses carries an increased credibility, since the witnesses are the ones who hold, in greater depth, the knowledge of the mystery of God revealed in Jesus Christ, which is made present in the world through the Spirit dwelling within their bodies and lives.

A witness is someone deeply torn in flesh and spirit. Witnesses are

---

1. See Hebrews 4:12.

2. See Jon Sobrino, *Extra pauper nulla salus* (Madrid: Trotta, 2009), 13 (Eng. trans., *No Salvation outside the Poor* (Maryknoll, NY: Orbis Books, 2008).

3. We adopt here the concept of "liquid" adopted by Zygmunt Bauman in many of his books: see, e.g., Zygmunt Bauman, *Liquid Life* (Cambridge: Polity Press, 2005); Zygmunt Bauman, *Liquid Modernity* (Cambridge: Polity Press, 2000); and Zygmunt Bauman, *Liquid Love: On the Frailty of Human Bonds* (Cambridge: Polity Press, 2003). By "liquid," he means without consistency, frail, ephemeral.

torn first within the self, between the highest point of their thirst for truth and transcendence on the one hand and the limited individual beings whose lives they inhabit temporally. The witness is torn by this gulf that still separates the truth to which he or she testifies from the world, which does not want to receive the message.[4]

According to Jean-Philippe Pierron, the *exalted* human being of modernity, autonomous and glorious, was crushed by totalitarian ideologies. Nazism, communism, and its byproducts—all of which wanted to change the human being radically and collectively—are very vivid in recent memory. Because of those ideologies, the *humiliated* human being emerged in society. This is one who is subject to the relentless requirement of a new destination for humanity. He or she does not rely anymore on his or her own capacity for initiative or power to innovate freely. Subject to the globalized economy, to laws of the market, to the dictatorship of consumerism, efficiency, beauty, pleasure, and much more, he or she finds little room for maneuvering to rediscover the path to authentic identity and human dignity.[5]

Between the *exalted* and the *humbled* human being, Pierron situates the witness, whom he calls the *fragilized* person. These are persons who, with lucidity, give up dreams of omnipotence but do not abdicate their identity or capacity for initiative. The originality and the irreplaceable value of these witnesses resides in the fact that their testimony—which they cannot fail to give and offer to the world, their contemporaries, and even to the whole of human history—is something that connects inseparably the content of their narrative to a way of being and existing; this is a mode of being that mobilizes all human capacities, whether in word, attitudes, or in resistance.[6]

Therefore, witnesses are always discomforting, embarrassing, and disturbing, as they call up something radical and *excessive*. And this is the mystery that underlies the human condition as such. This mystery stands in opposition to any attempt to reduce, attack, or minimize it, because the witness is someone who has experienced the Absolute

---

4. See Arthur Adamov, "Avertissement," in Rainer Maria Rilke, *Le livre de la pauvreté et de la mort*, trans. Arthur Adamov (Paris: Actes Sud, 1982), 7; cited in the epigraph of Jean-Philippe Pierron, *Le passage de temoin: Une philosophie du témoignage* (Paris: Editions du Cerf, 2006), 9.

5. See Pierron, *Le passage,* 16.

6. Ibid., 17.

and has made this experience the guiding principle of his or her life. In this sense, witnesses and their narratives infiltrate, so to speak, the volatility and ethereality of the world. In doing so, witnesses take truth for a biography, to the extent that it becomes their life story. Witnesses expose themselves to the boldness of employing a new logic and a new language by which to pronounce the Absolute, the truth for which humanity has an unquenchable thirst.

The witness is thus someone vulnerable, exposed, and surrendered to the world and to others in full readiness. Fully relational in character, witnesses attest to something they have seen, heard, or touched with their own hands, a foundational experience in their lives. Moreover, this experience does not belong to them alone, but also to others. In this sense, witnesses are figures who mediate conflicts in order to help bring forth dialogues otherwise seemingly impossible. They are also dependent figures at the service of the Absolute and the truth, that is, voluntarily abdicating themselves in order to mediate truth.[7] They attest to more than their own person. They bear a truth that cannot be reduced to mere opinion. The testimony of the witness is subjectively verifiable and sufficient. This gives his or her testimony a kind of normativity, since the destiny of the witness is inseparable from the truth.[8]

The witness, therefore, is comparable to what the history of ideas has called a *hero*, a category that, together with the saint and the scholar, serves to classify the moral attitudes required by the human condition.[9] The hero serves a self-surpassing cause. He or she is distinguished not by a dynamism of soul and energy of character but by the greatness and nobility present in the existential options he or she makes in life.[10]

Where will we find today those witnesses who tell us that it is still worth struggling for truth, justice, and peace? Where can they be found? We think that our contemporary mystics can be these heroes: different, discrete, and humble, present where anyone would want to

---

7. On this, see Emmanuel Levinas, *Autrement qu'être ou au-delà de l'essence* (La Haye: Martinus Nijhoff, 1974).

8. Pierron, *Le passage*, 23.

9. See "Sainteté." *Encyclopædia universalis*, http://www.universalis.fr/encyclopedie/saintete/; see also André-Jean Festugière, *La sainteté* (Paris: Presses universitaires de France, 1949).

10. Ibid.

be, going where nobody wants to go, and burning with a flame that never fades. These men and women are fragile and *excessive,* exposed and willing to die for the truth they have experienced, and to which they are eager to bear witness to their contemporaries.

One does not need to go to the confinement of the cloister to find them. They can be found on the streets in our large cities, at the borders and the periphery of the world, and in places that are difficult and *ugly,* according to our aesthetic standards. They may also be found in *dangerous* places that make us tremble in fear.

These contemporary mystics are witnesses to the mystery that drew them in and with which they have consented to enter into intimate communion. They attest to everything they have seen, heard, touched and learned, making available their *knowledge,* which is, after all, *love.*[11] From the fruition of this mystical union, the heroes of divine intimacy embrace peacefully and joyfully the risk and danger of witness in the public square. The ardor of their zeal irresistibly impels them to meet threats, conflicts, and even violent death.

Indeed, the history and etymology of the English word "testimony" reveal something important about the nature and identity of the witness. It is a word that is inseparable from the history of martyrdom, understood from the beginning as testimony through the shedding of blood. In Greek, the word "witness" is *martys,* "martyr," having less a legal meaning than an anthropological aspect.[12]

---

11. In the Bible, "to know" is inseparable from "to love." The word is used in reference to sexual relationships. The husband "knows" the wife in the intimacy of the nuptial chamber, etc. (see Genesis 4:1, 17, 25, among others).

12. The Greek word *martus* comes from the root *mrtu,* from which derives also the Greek *merméra,* "anguish, care, concern," and also the Greek *mermērizo,* "to be busy, concerned." The underlying Indo-European root is *smer (mer),* which means "to think, to reflect, to recall, to remember." *Smrti,* in Sanskrit, means "that which is remembered, is surrendered to memory, that is, to tradition." Understanding the etymology and history of the word, we arrive at the following description: *marturia,* "testimony," is the act or the consequence of giving witness, of testifying, that is, an act of deposition that has force and value in itself, for which we are concerned, that we remember, and for which we feel anxiety and anguish. Cf. Pierron, *Le passage,* 21, citing Raimon Panikkar, "Témoignage et dialogue," in *Le témoignage, actes du colloque organisé par le Centre international d'études humanistes et par l'Institut d'études philosophiques de Rome,* ed. E. Castelli (Paris: Aubier-Montaigne, 1972), 367-88, at 373.

Mysticism nowadays is therefore characterized by its indissoluble ties with ethics and all that derives from it, namely, transformative action in the world, political commitment, dialogue with other religious experiences, and the alliance with a conflict-ridden and suffering world. This is a constitutive element of mysticism's synthesis and a powerful criterion for its authenticity, for mysticism is the cradle of testimony.

Without this connection to the realm of ethics, talk of mysticism may generate fears of an alienating spiritual intimacy, an abandonment of the primacy of a transformative praxis ingrained in history.[13] This is a danger that haunts Christianity today, as we are regularly disenchanted by the failing of paradigms—whether political or otherwise.[14]

It is well known that the motif of a mysticism of action, of spirituality closely linked to a transformative undertaking, is occurring inside the *polis*. It was present in the liberation theology that emerged in Latin America, particularly in the now-classic and pioneering book by Gustavo Gutiérrez in the early 1970s.[15] However, even prior to this, a mysticism was already present in the action, thought, and words of many men and women, clergy and laity, Catholic and Protestant, for whom the experience of God awakened an ineluctable need to connect the experience of God with the pursuit of justice.

The German Jesuit Karl Rahner made a decisive contribution to this in contemporary theology. His major concern was to help modern people to believe. Engaged in a dialogue with nonbelievers, he built his theology on two principles. The first principle was to bring out the nature of fundamental human experience. This would serve as a basis of understanding from which to proceed in dialogue. The

---

13. Cf. liberation theology and its critique of the immobilizing alienation of a certain kind of spirituality.

14. See João Batista Libanio, "Mística e missão do professor," *Informativo* SBC, April 8, 2009, http://www.infosbc.org.br/portal/index.php?option=com_content &view=article&id=364:mistica-e-missao-do-professor-por-j-b-libanio&catid= 79:funcao&Itemid=97.

15. See Gustavo Gutiérrez, *Teologia da libertação* (Petrópolis: Vozes, 1975). See also Pedro Casaldáliga and José Maria Vigil, *Espiritualidade da libertação*, 2d ed. (Petrópolis: Vozes, 1993), especially the section "Constantes da espiritualidade da libertação," 228ff.

second was to recognize the identity particular to each party in the dialogue. The believer feels and thinks as a believer; the nonbeliever feels and thinks as a nonbeliever.

Karl Rahner did not imagine that an individual raises the question of God in the abstract; on the contrary, he wanted to formulate his theology by setting out from the human being as such. He tried to maintain a close connection between all that is fundamental to the human being and to Christianity. A human being carries in him- or herself a great question: the question of what it truly means to be human. What Christianity has to say in response constitutes an answer to what is constitutive in being human. Rahner's work sets out to demonstrate that, in thinking about faith, one must take into account both the internal experience of faith and the demands and problems of the modern world. Only when we do this can we produce a theology that facilitates the encounter with Jesus Christ for men and women today and for all times. Rahner's theology helpfully links mysticism with ethics in order to make mysticism intelligible today.

Johann Baptist Metz is one of the most brilliant disciples of Rahner and the founder of the so-called school of political theology, which strongly influenced liberation theology in Latin America. At a certain point, Metz moved away from his master's transcendental theology to develop a practical fundamental theology. Metz makes, in his work, constant reference to his own experience. It is easier, therefore, to more deeply understand his thought, because, as Metz maintains, even in treating the topic of God the theologian cannot avoid his or her own biography.

Metz says that it is important to be a mystic with eyes open to the world in order to perceive its challenges and to feel its sufferings and conflicts.[16] In one of his recent works, *Memoria passionis*, he looks for ways to respond to the following question: in the face of the innocent victims of injustice is there a criterion of understanding and binding coexistence that can be recognized as true for all?[17] The key terms in formulating an answer are, according to Metz, on the one hand, the

---

16. See Johann-Baptist Metz, *El clamor de la tierra: El problema dramático de la teodicea* (Estella: Verbo Divino, 1996), 26.

17. See Johann-Baptist Metz, *Memoria passionis: Una evocación provocadora en una sociedad pluralista* (Santander: Sal Terrae, 2007).

subversive memory of the victims—a memory that makes them active again in history—and, on the other hand, *compassion*.[18]

Compassio is not merely an interior consciousness from above or outside, but a sense of the suffering of others in which we are obliged to participate. This kind of compassion merits the categorical imperative: "stop, listen and look."[19] Moreover, we should add, "and tell others about what you have seen, heard, and touched." *Compassio* is the ability to share the suffering of others. Indeed, the most terrible aspect of suffering is not so much the pain itself but the loneliness therein. Metz's project is to develop a *memoria passionis* as the basic category for theology in the public square. It consists in the remembrance of others' sufferings—a public recalling of others' suffering, integrated with reflection in such way that it becomes an indelible seal. From here, Metz believes, there arises the need for a new political theology that contributes vigorously to a church of *compassio*, in which the *memoria passionis* becomes a provocative basis for a new ethics.

The *memoria passionis*—the ground of a new ethics—sets out from the mysticism of open eyes taught and lived by Jesus in the face of others' suffering and pain. It is this spirit of *compassion* that necessarily makes a mystic become a witness. Witnesses cannot *but* tell others about what they have seen and heard. In addition, the witness can help to transform that reality only by transforming his or her own action.

It is this spirit of compassion that seizes today's mystics, sending them boldly toward an encounter with political, social, and cultural conflicts. Thus, the mystical experience supports its claim to authenticity as an experience of God by appealing to the authority of those who suffer—an authority that challenges and is accessible to all human beings. This authority of those who suffer is that interior authority of a global ethos, a universal morality, that would empower any person, independent of any ideology or any point of view. It is a morality that cannot be put aside or relativized by any culture or any religion or church. True mysticism today, especially after Auschwitz, cannot *but* be inspired by that ethos. In addition, politics, inspired by this ethos, would certainly be more humanizing.

---

18. Ibid., 36-39: "La mística del sufrimiento enrazón de Dius."

19. Ibid., 160-83: "El programa del cristianismo para el mundo en medio del pluralism de religions y culturas: la 'compassio.'"

Spirituality and mysticism, therefore, represent an attitude that is alert, vigilant, with open eyes to see, read, and understand reality, and then to testify about it and transform it according to the Spirit of God. This is a concrete way, moved by the Spirit, to live the gospel. It is an authentic way to live before God in solidarity with everyone, especially the poor and oppressed.[20]

It is possible therefore to assert that mysticism can find its origin and its environment in the *interruption* that stimulates compassion for others' poverty and pain. All of the movement here described is not only ethical but also mystical—or rather, because it is mystical, it is ethical and vice versa; as in biblical revelation, the two are not dissociated.

All human praxis is subject to certain criteria. Political praxis can be seen as an outflow of the self that may be likened to an experience of ecstasy. To live in a spirit of compassion is to immerse oneself in the other, in his or her disfigured and suffering reality, identifying with it, sympathizing with it, and in entering into communion with it in order to denounce it and allow for its transformation. If the ecstasies of the mystics are justly recognized by official religion, they are not the most important criteria for assessing the authenticity of their experience; rather, it is the concrete works, the fruits that follow upon the ecstasies, that denote the degree of authenticity.

The life of the mystic is therefore an exodus, which, as a kind of standing apart from one's self, is the same as an ecstasy. Facing the otherness of God, who inspires the mystic and fills her with joy and wonder, the mystic moves toward the neighbor, in order to serve. The experience of union with God characteristic of mysticism is far from being a grace-filled realization of the delights and wonders of the contemplation of the eternal mysteries. It is, primarily, a sending into the world and the assumption of responsibility in relation to others. If the word *mysticism* or *mystical* is rooted in the word *mystery,* then the mystical experience means, in short, an experience of intimacy with mystery. It is a mystery of responsibility in which the mystic responds to others, and experiences in his or her flesh the consequences and weight of an evil that he or she did not cause, while at the same time

---

20. Gustavo Gutiérrez, *Beber no próprio poço* (Petrópolis: Vozes, 1984), 107ff. (Eng. trans., *We Drink from Our Own Wells* (Maryknoll, NY: Orbis Books, 1984, 2003).

accepting insertion within a cooperative, redemptive economy that he or she did not invent and over which the mystic does not preside.

Contemporary mystics who have lived a *theo-pathic* experience— an experience of being passionately configured by divine love and union with the mystery—are fit mediators to proclaim today who God is. In addition, they are also empowered by God to announce it in the midst of a secular world that seems to have lost the language to speak about God. As well as being mystics, they are witnesses to the Absolute, which they have experienced in their own lives. Their testimony is a form of mediation through which the divine now tries to speak and express itself in the midst of the world.[21]

Again, Metz says that the mystical experience involves an intensive perception of the other's pain; it is being a "*mystic with open eyes.*"[22] Surely, Metz refers here to the etymology of the word *mysticism*, which comes from the Greek verb *myō*, "to close, shut up," or "shut the mouth or eyes." He goes beyond this, stating that mysticism within the Judeo-Christian tradition is rather mysticism with open eyes. The mystical experience thus consists not so much in having extraordinary visions but in having *a new vision of all reality*, discovering God as the vision's ultimate truth, as its living foundation, active and ever new.

The mystic with open eyes sees all reality, knowing that the final dimension of all reality is inhabited by someone, by God. This mystic never tires of contemplating life but always seeks the face of God. Diving into human situations, torn or happy, he or she looks for that presence of God who acts, giving life and freedom. Already the scholastics claimed that mysticism is *fides oculata*, a faith endowed with eyes, that is, an illuminated faith through which it is possible to see reality in the light of God.[23]

This seems to describe the mystics of today, those who, in the desert of secularism, seek God's footprints in history. They move through the mystery of an encounter with God where their impurities and weaknesses are purified. They are thereby increasingly enfolded into the intimacy of an endless loving union. What they contemplate, clos-

---

21. See Pierron, *Le passage*, 30.

22. See Metz, *El clamor*, 26.

23. See Raimon Panikkar, *De la mística: Experiencia plena de la vida* (Barcelona: Herder, 2005), 53.

ing their eyes and immersing themselves in interior prayer, allows them to see with transfigured eyes the conflictive reality of humanity, their vision purified of prejudice and discrimination.[24]

To the contemplative eyes of the mystic, there is no profane reality, for God is present everywhere, as a loving and freeing presence. Becoming aware of this presence and experiencing it as love, the mystic bears witness, gives testimony, reveals this truth to others and joins God's liberating action.[25]

Facing the pain and harshness of reality, these mystics with open eyes see what is not evident or obvious, committing themselves to that seed of life that seems smothered by death and destruction. This fills them with a hope that appears to the world to be foolish and dangerous. Emerging from interior illumination while seeking contact with the loving mystery of God, the mystic, now with open eyes, sees everything in a different light, with a new lucidity, with true transparency, pregnant with life and hope.[26]

The primary source for the content of mystical experience is the testimony of the mystics themselves. They are the first and most important theoreticians of that experience.[27] The biography of the believer is the condition of the possibility for a theological reading of mystical experience and its testimony in today's world. This is true to the extent that the believer's biography, along with its concrete configuration, receives its existence from God, being inaugurated with the event of God in his or her life; it is also true to the extent that the narrative manifests itself as a history of *salvation*, a concrete *exegesis* of faith.[28]

Many contemporary theologians underline, with increasing frequency, the importance of passing from a rigidly speculative theology to a narrative theology, where mysteries can be *told*, narrated, and

---

24. See Benjamin Gonzalez Buelta, *Caminar sobre las aguas* (Santander: Sal Terrae, 2011). .

25. Ibid.

26. Ibid.

27. See Henrique Claudio de Lima Vaz, *Experiencia mística e filosofia na tradição occidental* (São Paulo: Loyola, 2000).

28. On this, see the small but valuable book by Michael Schneider, *Teologia como biografia: Una fundamentación dogmatica* (Bilbao: Desclée, 2000), esp. 22.

only then subjected to reflection.[29] At present, there is also a growing emphasis on the importance of doing theology not only from texts but also from witnesses.[30]

Theology is, to some extent, obliged to carry out its reflection from within the act of following Jesus; it may be called "theology" only when this action establishes the proper starting point for reflection.[31] When this happens, then the *reading* of the lives of the witnesses—mystics, prophets, and saints—will be something equivalent to the personal revelation of God, who is writing with the Spirit in the body and life of those who bear witness to God. Theological thinking, then, is not concerned with God as external object. It is rather God who reinforces and communicates with human thought, through the *ecstasies* of an existence informed and inspired by faith.[32]

Theological knowledge is not something to be communicated primarily and only through concepts but through the *event* of following Jesus, that is, through the biographies and the testimony of men and women who fall in love and experience this love as it is understood and proclaimed by the gospel of Jesus. Their experiences and lives will then consist of announcing the gospel through their own joyful and fruitful existences, and often also by their suffering and death. Their experience of faith confers to theology, then, a valuable and original configuration of praxis and narrative.[33]

---

29. See, for instance, the works of J. B. Metz, *Memoria passionis,* and Joseph Moingt, *L'homme qui venait de Dieu* (Paris: Cerf, 2001); Joseph Moingt, *Dieu qui vient a l'homme,* 2 vols. (Paris: Cerf, 2002, 2007), among others. The same reflection is made by Jon Sobrino, departing from the perspective of his own theology, "not of texts, but of witnesses" ("no de textos sino de testigos").

30. This is also supported by *Evangelii nuntiandi* §41, where Pope Paul VI says, "Modern man listens more willingly to witnesses than to teachers, and if he does listen to teachers, it is because they are witnesses." See http://www.vatican.va/holy_father/paul_vi/apost_exhortations/documents/hf_p-vi_exh_19751208_evangelii-nuntiandi_en.html.

31. Michael Schneider, *Teologia como biografia,* 24.

32. Ibid., n. 16.

33. See Johann-Baptist Metz, *A fé em história e em sociedade: Estudos para uma teologia fundamental prática* (São Paulo: Paulinas, 1980).

2

Giving Witness, Receiving Testimony

Michael L. Budde

Introduction

One breaks no new ground in observing an exaggerated sense of individualism in many understandings of witness and testimony. Both in formal hagiographies and in popular venerations of prophetic and heroic persons, considerable emphasis rests on the moral courage and determination of individuals and the message they proclaim or affirm.

At another level, of course, there is the recognition that witness is fundamentally a communal phenomenon. It is an interplay between giving witness and receiving testimony, an ongoing process in which reception itself defines and constructs testimony; it is a dialectic in which testimony both identifies and challenges the roles of those who testify and those who receive testimony.

We gather today in part to remember the witness of our Salvadoran brothers and sisters whose lives were and are a testimony to the goodness of God and God's hopes for his creation. We gather to reflect on the martyrdom forced upon them, and upon many like them, in a world in which good news is bad news to be suppressed and silenced. And we gather to ask whether and how those of us still on this part of life's journey can learn from the testimony of others and in the process become more adequate witnesses to the God of the poor who seeks to make all things new and whose kingdom has already begun for those with eyes to see and ears to hear.

In these remarks, I hope not so much to reflect on the giving of witness and testimony but instead to reflect on the *reception* of this witness and testimony. It is my contention that problems of reception and receptivity draw our attention to certain deficiencies of church life and practice and invite a rethinking of certain aspects of ecclesiology if the church is to more adequately be part of the "cloud of witnesses" (Hebrews 12:1) that expresses Christ's life in and for the world. Doing so is worthwhile, I hope, not merely to provide a conceptual corrective to excessively individualized notions of witness and testimony but also to suggest how proclaiming the radical gospel of Christ seems to entail communal practices and dispositions of an everyday, often overlooked, sort. Public witness and testimony, I suggest, are built on humble and often unseen practices of the *ekklēsia* seeking to practice discipleship in a world of many messages, countless testimonials, and contradictory witnesses.

Witness as Both Pitch and Catch

Scripture scholar Nadine Pence Frantz reminds us of the centrality of testimony as a central form in a healthy interpretation of the Bible. She describes testimony as

> a narrative of a people whose self-perception was primarily defined by its interaction with God . . . the intent of the whole [Bible] is testimonial, including a rhetorical function designed to evoke a response of appropriation. In other words, "Scripture is seen as that which was told and recorded with the intent to evoke a similar life and faith in other people. It is intended to evoke an encounter."[1]

Testimony, witness, martyrdom—all require persons formed by encounter with the Jesus of the gospels, the kingdom promises of the Hebrew Bible, and the Holy Spirit as enfleshed in the lives of earlier witnesses and exemplars. Such is more than a simple transmission-belt notion of communication (sender-message-receiver), or some similarly mechanistic notion of information conveyance or data-encoding/transmission/decoding; we are not talking about e-mail or texting, in other words. In fact, it is the matter of "formation," no

---

1. Nadine Pence Frantz, "Biblical Interpretation in a 'Non-Sense' World: Text, Revelation, and Interpretive Community," *Brethren Life and Thought* 39.3 (1994): 153-66, at 158.

longer the province of religious life, that stands as perhaps the crucial center for thinking theologically and ecclesially about witness and testimony in varied contexts and circumstances.

Put simply, "being a Christian" means among other things that one's imagination, desires, perceptions, standards, and ways of encountering the world are shaped by the stories, images, songs, categories, and norms of Jesus, of his followers and antecedents in the Hebrew Bible. One learns from the elders in the faith who have given this narrative hands and feet and tears and smiles and lessons and laughter and struggle—the grandmothers and aunts, fathers and cousins, and those who are the cloud of witnesses in the everyday life of the Christian way.

This is some of what is meant by being "transformed by the renewal of your mind" (Romans 12:2, ESV), which too often is reduced to a cognitive or knowledge-based sensibility that focuses too much on propositions, dogma, and intellect. More adequately understood, the formation of Christian communities and members when done well is a holistic process of conversion, a joint venture of the Holy Spirit and the *ekklēsia* through which new Christians are made. To the extent that we Christians engage life with imaginations and minds and habits attuned to the good news of Christ, to that extent are we the products of processes of craft formation (rather than industrial mass production).

In one sense, the formation of Christians is comparable to the other formative processes by which persons and communities are formed—indeed, rival processes of formation are the rule in most times and places, with different (and sometimes antagonistic) structures and processes seeking to shape human affections, dispositions, and desires. The cultural ecologies of capitalism, the socializing imperatives of nationalism, the identity constructions of white supremacy—these are just a few of the formative rivals to Christianity in our time and place, inasmuch as they cultivate and shape toward ends far from the kingdom of God as exemplified in the Sermon on the Mount (which John Paul II called the "Magna Carta" of the Christian movement).

It takes a special kind of person and a special kind of community to see "loving one's enemies" as good news, to understand "repaying evil with good" as how one should act, to encounter the creator of the universe in the person of the destitute, the neglected, or the oppressed. These are not "natural" perceptions, far from where the natural law however construed leads, and definitely at odds with the world constructed and maintained by capital, the state, and other formative powers.

Given that the concept of Christian formation extends beyond the realm of religious and clergy to include all the baptized, and given that the practices of Christianity (worship, prayer, work on behalf of justice, life with and for the poor, study and fellowship) are required for the sustenance and adaptation of Christianity across time and contexts, the processes of testimony and witness presuppose formation done with a minimum degree of adequacy. For ours is a faith handed on from others, a simple-yet-complex bundle that we receive before we change it and hand it on, something that comes first "from hearing" (Romans 10:17) before it can be proclaimed.

If that is true, then being a people formed deeply by the stories of Jubilee and Jeremiah, of Jesus and Mary of Magdala, of the martyrs and the prophets, is necessary if one is to have witnesses, persons whose words and lives give testimony to God's plan for creation. We know this is true, and we hold up those exemplary witnesses who give us a glimpse of who and what God is, of what it means to forgive one's enemies and see God in those the world despises and ridicules. We give them names like Romero and Ellacuría, Daniel Berrigan and Dorothy Day, the martyrs of Uganda and of Japan, and many more.

Yet what is no less important but too easily overlooked is that each of these witnesses requires a community not only to form and send them but one capable of receiving their testimony. This is true of the testimony of word and deed, but especially true of that testimony unto death that the Christian tradition calls martyrdom. And this is where the tendency toward individualism limits our understanding of witness in our day—too much attention to those individuals, famous and unknown, whose lives speak the truth of God, and too little attention to those communities that receive their testimony, who become its caretakers and custodians, in whose hands it has been entrusted.

The stakes in all of this are significant. As Craig Hovey notes, the deaths of martyrs "are very often not the straightforward witness implied by words that paint an ideal picture."

> Martyrs cannot declare their own deaths to be martyr-deaths, and thus their ultimate risk is perhaps dying without any guarantee about how they will be remembered or whether they will

be remembered at all. In death, martyrs submit to the collective judgment of the church and put their own contribution to that judgment on the line. This is because silenced martyrs are not only unable to speak to their killers the testimony for which they died; they also are unable to speak within the church in ways that would help secure the significance of their own deaths.[2]

Where Christian formation has been done poorly, or in a superficial way, or been overwritten by the powerful formative dynamics of other claimants on human identity and allegiance, there will witness be inadequately proclaimed, received, sustained, or maintained. There exists an extensive and generally depressing literature on the failures of Christian formation among congregations in advanced industrial countries; historic and contemporary deficiencies among congregations in the global South are also well known among pastors and scholars alike. Indeed, substantial problems in Christian formation seem to be a common dilemma joining Catholic congregations worldwide, communities with otherwise very different contexts and circumstances.

Let us look at a few examples from one particular set of twentieth-century European contexts that I hope will illustrate the matter and allow for conversation across the divergent expressions of Catholic thought and practice in our own time.

The Reception of Witness

1. An Austrian Layman

On October 26, 2007, the Catholic bishop of Linz (Austria) and the archbishop of Innsbruck announced the formal beatification of Franz Jägerstätter, whom they described as a "martyr" and "a prophet with a global view and a penetrating insight."[3]

Jägerstätter's witness was of a straightforward nature: After returning home from basic military training in 1941, Jägerstätter vowed not to return, refusing to help advance the Nazi cause as a member of the

---

2. Craig Hovey, *Bearing True Witness: Truthfulness in Christian Practice* (Grand Rapids, MI: Eerdmans Publishing, 2011), 5-6.

3. Ludwig Schwarz and Manfred Scheuer, "Foreword," in Erna Putz, *Franz Jägerstätter—Martyr: A Shining Example in Dark Times* (Linz, Austria: Buchverlag Franz Steinmassl, 2007), 7.

Austrian military (Austria had been annexed by Germany in 1938). He considered Nazi Germany to be an evil regime wholly incompatible with Christianity, describing its wars as unjust plunder and the savaging of its neighbors, which his Christian conscience could not allow him to support in any way. Despite repeated efforts on all sides to convince him otherwise, Jägerstätter refused to change his mind; he was arrested and finally executed by beheading in 1943. In this we have a classic, almost stereotypical, story of brave Christian witness— a martyr like other shining examples in the twentieth century, held up by the church for veneration and imitation.

Well, not quite.

If Jägerstätter's testimony merited beatification by 2007, the church that produced him received his witness in an altogether different fashion. What Jägerstätter did, he did in the face of opposition from all sides—from his mother and wife and family, his friends and neighbors, his parish priest and bishop, and of course from his government leaders.

While Jägerstätter's position rested on the duty to follow Christ rather than an evil regime bent on the destruction of the innocent (as well as of the church), his pastors emphasized that such decisions were not the responsibility of lay persons. Rather, they were to obey civil authority in accord with Romans 13 and similar texts; they also emphasized Jägerstätter's duty to provide for his family, who would be made to suffer if he continued to refuse military service to the Nazis.

In his research on Jägerstätter, including interviews with his family and neighbors, North American sociologist Gordon Zahn described the general sense of the community about Jägerstätter, both during his lifetime and when his witness began gathering international attention after more than a decade of silence:

> The community continues to reject Jägerstätter's stand as a stubborn and pointless display of essentially political imprudence, or even an actual failure to fulfill a legitimate duty. It is to be explained and forgiven in terms of an unfortunate mental aberration brought about, or at least intensified, by religious excess. The question of whether his action was morally right is, for the most part, set aside. While some of the villagers were quite willing to accept the possibility that he might someday be formally acknowledged as a saint, this possibility was not considered at

all incompatible with the community's general disapproval of his action.[4]

Zahn notes that, for the most part, Jägerstätter's contemporaries tried to avoid talking or thinking about him—his story was not told to their children, and most seemed to hope the story would go away on its own.[5] When it came to Catholic leaders, Zahn notes that while "they could congratulate him for his unswerving commitment and give him assurances that he would not be committing a sin . . . none had been able or willing to tell him that *he was right*.[6] In fact, many in the Austrian hierarchy after the war had difficulty discussing Jägerstätter's case in ways that didn't reflect poorly on their support for the war effort.[7] Emblematic in this respect, to Zahn, was Bishop Joseph Fleisser of Linz, who after the war could describe Jägerstätter as a "martyr to conscience" but not as an example worthy of imitation.

> I consider the greatest heroes to be those exemplary young Catholic men, seminarians, priests, and heads of families who fought and died in heroic fulfillment of duty and in the firm conviction that they were fulfilling the will of God at their post just as the Christian soldiers in the armies of the heathen emperor had done.[8]

Similarly, the then–cardinal archbishop of Vienna was the influential Cardinal Innitzer, who signed his letters "Heil Hitler."[9] Jägerstätter's witness, in other words, was a seed that seemed to land on rocky Catholic soil of a most infertile sort.

2. Of Catholics and Jews

By many measures, one of the most dramatic changes in formal Catholic teaching in the past hundred years has been its understanding of

---

4. Gordon Zahn, *In Solitary Witness: The Life and Death of Franz Jägerstätter* (Springfield, IL: Templegate Publishers, 1964), 146.

5. Ibid., 146-48, 150.

6. Ibid., 162.

7. Ibid., 164-65.

8. Ibid.

9. John Connelly, *From Enemy to Brother: The Revolution in Catholic Teaching on the Jews, 1933-1965* (Cambridge, MA: Harvard University Press, 2012), 30-31.

and relationship to Judaism and the Jews. Centuries of enmity and competition, persecution and vilification, supersessionism and damnation—all of this and more typify Catholicism and its engagement with Judaism. How remarkable, indeed how unbelievable, must have been the pronouncements of *Nostra aetate*, the Vatican II declaration that marked a new day in Christianity and Judaism. In some respects this was among the most powerful and perhaps improbable of the fruits of Vatican II, marking as it did a category shift in the church's theological understanding of Judaism and the role of Judaism in Christian mission, thought, and practice.

But where did this dramatic shift come from? How did the orthodox Catholic rejection of Judaism that lasted until the 1960s undergo such a sea change, to the point where the Jews were no longer the "perfidious Jews" of the Passion liturgy but now our "elder brothers in the faith," as Pope John Paul II said in a December 31, 1986, homily? Jews no longer needed to be converted in order to be saved; God's covenant with the chosen people remains in force, and was not abrogated by the rejection of Jesus by the Jewish leadership of his day. The Jews were not Christ-killers, they did not murder Christian babies for their Passover rituals (the "blood libel" of immense power), and they were not rejected by God.

By itself, the horrors of the Holocaust seem insufficient to explain the change in Catholicism relative to Judaism; by themselves human atrocities rarely push events in a single, predetermined direction. From where did the new understanding of the Jews come, and how did it find reception in the formal teaching of the Catholic Church?

In the terms we are exploring in this essay, the ecclesial community was distinctly ill equipped (ill formed, in fact) to generate and receive a new word, a life-giving word, for the Jews from its own resources in the years up to Vatican II. So profoundly had Catholic imaginations, categories, and dispositions been formed by religious and secular notions of Jews as deficient that the prospects for a new witness seemed unpromising in the extreme. If Jägerstätter represented a church incapable of receiving testimony, Catholic attitudes toward the Jews reflected incapacities on both the sending and receiving ends of witness.

In this, one may commend a new book by John Connelly, a historian at the University of California at Berkeley. His 2012 book, *From*

Enemy to Brother: The Revolution in Catholic Teaching on the Jews, 1933-1965, is an enlightening and persuasive exploration of these and other questions.

The first thing one derives from reading Connelly's careful account is how unpromising were the prospects for a reversal of Christian antipathy—theological and political—toward the Jews. In this, he notes the importance of distinguishing between anti-Semitism (as a modern racial theory, positing a biological inferiority of the Jewish "race"), and anti-Judaism (as a Christian theological position "which foments contempt by considering the Jewish people cursed by God and carrying a special burden of suffering through history").[10]

These concepts, while distinct, often overlapped in Christian thought and practice to the point where anti-Jewish theological thinking limited and sometimes undermined Christian resistance to the "modern" racism of anti-Semitism.

> Even the most determined Christian opponents of Nazism—including Dietrich Bonhoeffer—shared with the anti-Semites the basic belief that Jews lived under a curse for killing Christ. That robbed them of the language with which to speak unequivocally in favor of Jews during the Holocaust. Nothing in the Christian tradition permitted them to understand Jewish suffering as other than divinely willed.[11]

This interaction of "scientific" racism and theological anti-Judaism created divides that even baptism was unable to erase, erecting barriers that Catholicism had to accept. As Connelly notes,

> In German-speaking Europe . . . Catholicism opened itself to racist theology after World War I, and priests and influential intellectuals told the Catholic faithful that Jews—that region's "racial other" by common consent—bore a second original sin, an *Erbsünde* signaling special propensity to evil, transmitted from generation to generation and not erased by baptism. . . . Once Jews entered the church, they had to be kept from high office and made to "work hard on themselves" over generations to undo the genetic inheritance of a supposed apostasy that

---

10. Ibid., 6.
11. Ibid., 9.

took place hundreds of years earlier. In effect, a Jew could not become a full-fledged Christian in his or her lifetime.[12]

While this may sound strange to us today, contradicting the power of baptism to create a new people and erase distinctions between them (neither Gentile nor Jew, slave nor free, as Galatians 3:28 reads), Connelly notes that "German theologians of the prewar era believed they faced another 'fact': that human races composed part of the natural order, and that these races consisted of persons having shared characteristics. Given that the church derives its ethics from natural law, the question then became how to adapt moral teaching to what seemed to be the realm of nature."[13]

The "best of natural science" proved to be the path of anti-Semitism into Catholic thought in Germany, where it met with the near-universal Catholic anti-Judaism whose reach extended far beyond culturally German lands. The results flowered in the work of the two premier Catholic voices on Catholicism and race in Germany. The first of these was developmental biologist and Jesuit priest Hermann Muckermann, director of the eugenics section at the Kaiser Wilhelm Institute for Anthropology in Berlin and author of more than 250 works on eugenics, families, heredity, and the like (his work on race alone went through thirty editions). In a major work published as the Nazis were entering into power, Muckermann wrote,

> Our first concern is to maintain the untouched, hereditary, elemental nature of the German people. . . . The present age, which desires the renewal of the German people from its deepest biological sources, causes us to direct particular attention to this goal. One cause for concern is without doubt the swelling numbers of persons of Jewish origin in essential branches of our cultural life.[14]

In the context of his time in Catholic circles, Connelly notes, "he was not seen as a racist."

The other great Catholic voice on race during this period was Father Wilhelm Schmidt, a Society of the Divine Word priest at the

---

12. Ibid., 12.

13. Ibid.

14. Quoted in ibid., 15.

University of Vienna. He so impressed Pius XI that the pope helped finance a museum of ethnology for him at the Vatican; because of its emphasis on culture and spirituality over physics and materialism, Schmidt was considered a more "moderate" voice on science and Christianity.[15] Connelly notes that

> Schmidt had all the scientific legitimacy of Muckermann and ... he and his students controlled appointments in the discipline for decades.... Like Muckermann, Schmidt proceeded from an a priori belief in a hierarchy of human races. In his view races had arisen as a result of environmental conditions, and once they cohered in natural history they took on a value that was transcendent.[16]

One of the environmental conditions of contemporary interest was the effects that killing Jesus had on the Jews, forever marking them as an alien race in Europe. As Schmidt noted,

> This kind of transgression can by itself distort the being of a people; yet in the case of the Jewish people, the betrayal of its high calling has made this distortion go very deep. In punishment this people, as Christ himself predicted, was driven out of its homeland. Almost two thousand years of distortion and uprooting of its essence has then had a secondary but real effect on its physical race. These racial effects ... are not neutralized by baptism. For that, Jews will have to work hard on themselves. [Converted Jews] may therefore belong to our number, but not in the same way as our German racial comrades.[17]

The risk one runs in using cases drawing upon German Catholicism at mid-century is that they are too easily written off as abnormal, as outliers and extremes with little relevance for Catholic thought and practice elsewhere. Time constraints forbid a full discussion here, but suffice to say I disagree with this view; German Catholicism continues to be relevant to the church universal for its strengths as well as its all-too-apparent weaknesses. Connelly is among many who draw

---

15. Ibid., 16.
16. Ibid., 16-17.
17. Ibid., 17.

attention to the vitality of German Catholicism, calling it "the most cohesive Catholic milieu in Europe," capable of producing "not only uniformed youth legions, but also newspapers and journals, trade unions, and the most powerful Catholic political organization in the world after the Vatican, the German Center Party."[18]

One could go on, and Connelly does, noting the influence of progressive Catholic theologians such as Karl Adam, for whom "discrimination against Jews did not contradict Christ's basic commandment to love one's neighbor as oneself. After all, love of the other assumed love of the self, and the self was German and Christian. He therefore portrayed Nazi-orchestrated boycotts of Jewish businesses as the fulfillment of Christian charity, acts of Christian-German 'self-assertion' aimed at stemming the 'Jewish deluge.'"[19] No fringe voice in the Catholic world, Adam's admirers have included Edward Schillebeeckx, Bernard Häring, Yves Congar, George Orwell, Dorothy Day, Flannery O'Connor, Karl Rahner, Karl Barth, Thomas Merton, Hans Küng, James Carroll, Pope Paul VI, and Pope Benedict XVI.[20] In other words, not even the best and brightest in the German church were of help in getting past Christian racism toward the Jews, and theological enmity toward them.

The literature on Catholicism and anti-Semitism (not to mention anti-Judaism) is huge, extensive, and generally depressing. Controversies abound among those who hold up the real but limited efforts of Catholics in the face of racial thinking and policy, and those who are more fundamentally convinced of the church's accommodation and facilitation of such structures and beliefs. Resolving those disputes is not our business here, but even so it remains a puzzle. Given the depth and breadth of anti-Jewish theology and pastoral practice, popular beliefs, and prejudices, from where could a new testimony come? Who could bear witness to a vision of the Jews as a people to be loved as they are and not as aliens to be subdued, subordinated, or drowned in the distinctly gentile waters of baptism?

Those who did bear witness, inside and outside of Germanic Europe, and those who ultimately played the leading role in the creation of *Nostra aetate*, all shared a remarkable legacy, according to

---

18. Ibid., 68.
19. Ibid., 20.
20. Ibid., 21.

Connelly. They were converts, not cradle Catholics—not born into the mix of nation and religion that saturated the formation of Catholicism throughout Europe. Some of these witnesses were converts from Protestantism, like Karl Thieme. But the majority, those whose work would change the direction of Catholicism's view of Judaism, were themselves converts from Judaism and Jewish families. For those who know the history of Jewish-Catholic relations in the era before and after Vatican II, the list is a "who's who" of important theologians, pastors, and scholars: John Oesterreicher, who, with fellow converts of Jewish background Bruno Hussar and Gregory Baum, drafted *Nostra aetate*.[21] Others playing leading roles included Albert Fuchs, Maximilian Beck, Hans Zacharias, Walter Berger, Rudolf Lammel, and Dietrich von Hildebrand;[22] if one goes back just a bit farther in time, say to the 1840s, the list of converts, mostly from Jewish backgrounds, would include Leon Bloy, Raïssa Maritain, Erik Peterson, Waldemar Gurian, Paul Demann, Geza Vermes, and many others.[23]

All of this leads to Connelly's conclusion, relevant to our concern for witness and its reception: "Without converts, the Catholic Church would never have 'thought its way' out of the challenges of racist anti-Judaism." To him, the converts teach a lesson about solidarity, inasmuch as "it turned out [i.e., in Connelly's study] that virtually all of the Catholics concerned about protecting the 'other' were people Catholics in central Europe considered 'others.'"[24]

As Connelly notes, he started with the

> modest goal of answering the largely unexplored question of how the Holocaust changed the way Catholics thought about Jews. Contrary to widespread assumptions, the revolutionary about-face that took place at Vatican II did not flow "naturally" or "automatically" from reflections about the genocide, but rather resulted from struggle among theologians extending from the 1930s to the 1960s: about how to revise centuries of teaching on the crowd's self-deprecation in Matthew 27 ("let his blood be upon us and our children!"), or the place in the

---

21. Ibid., 7.
22. Ibid., 63-64.
23. Ibid., 287-88.
24. Ibid., 290.

Epistle to the Hebrews declaring God's covenant with the Jews obsolete, or the idea flowing from Matthew 28:19 that Christians had no option but to proselytize Jews. How could a priest who had preached one interpretation of the New Testament for decades suddenly reverse himself and still seem a source of reliable understanding of scripture?[25]

In highlighting the role of converts in breaking through an ecclesial culture too closely tied to its national culture, Connelly describes these voices as "perhaps the least cynical of Catholics, and [their] idealism led them to hone a sense of the practical."[26] He later continues this line:

We will never fully understand why this motley group converted to Catholicism. The decisions were individual. . . . Like other converts, they felt specially touched by grace: conversion involved embracing a mission from God, and one's life had to be visibly new. We see in John Oesterreicher, but also Dietrich von Hildebrand and Karl Thieme, not only passion but obsessive fervor; not only involvement but extraordinary commitment based not simply in belief but unwavering conviction; not only disinterest in popularity but insistence upon influence. Conversion had involved not just willingness to accept but courage to refuse, and therefore a readiness to defend unpopular positions. Many people are tempted to leave secure communities of origin—religious or otherwise—but converts are those who have summoned the conviction to do so, and it was belief rather than doubt that characterized them.[27]

Some Modest Conclusions:
Two Lessons on Receiving Testimony

It may seem as though I have wandered from my original intent to focus on how the formation of Christian affections, dispositions, and identities done poorly impedes not only the generation of gospel-centered testimony but also its reception. The cases I have described

25. Ibid., 10.
26. Ibid., 288.
27. Ibid.

here may seem too particular, too extreme, and too parochial to be of much value in thinking more broadly about the imperative of Christian witness from and to the numerous and varied contexts of the contemporary world. After all, what has Berlin to say to Belem, or Germany to Guatemala, or Salzburg to Salvador?

I am not alone in maintaining that testimony in general, and martyrdom in particular, requires the existence of a church or community capable of receiving witness—to name and affirm it, reflect upon and disseminate it, to employ it as a model of Christianity well lived that is taught to others. In the case of Jägerstätter, we have a rather curious martyr, one whose witness was, as Zahn notes, "a stand *against* his fellow Catholics and their spiritual leaders who were wholeheartedly committed to, or at least willing to acquiesce in, the war effort."[28] This powerful and improbable witness dramatized what one English bishop (during the Vatican II discussion of what would become the "Pastoral Constitution on the Church in the Modern World," *Gaudium et spes*) described as "the major scandal of Christianity," namely, that "almost every national hierarchy in almost every war has allowed itself to become the moral arm of its own government, even in wars later recognized as palpably unjust."[29] How ironic it is, then, that the successors to Jägerstätter's nationalist bishop would be those describing Jägerstätter as "a prophet with a global view and a penetrating insight . . . an advocate of non-violence and peace."[30]

It may be fair to say that the church's about-face on this Austrian farmer testifies to the indispensability of Christian universalism in allowing God to somehow redeem even the most seemingly useless of gospel-based witness. Had Jägerstätter's case not come to the attention of the church worldwide, thanks largely to the scholarly work of the late Gordon Zahn—had his memory remained within the confines of the Austrian church alone, in other words—it is hard to see this parish sacristan as someone who would later be praised and a martyr and candidate for sainthood. The first lesson to consider might be here: it took the larger church—transnational, not beholden to a single set of national allegiances or commitments—to recognize and receive this martyr's witness. Such may well be a structural commonplace in the era after

---

28. Zahn, *Solitary Witness*, 162-63.

29. Cited in "Preface," ibid., ii.

30. Schwarz and Scheuer, "Foreword," in Putz, *Franz Jägerstätter*, 7.

modernity, with the worldwide character of the body of Christ sliced into national fragments; tied so closely in many places to nationalist fusions of faith and political identity, such churches may be less capable of receiving witness and recognizing martyrdom in their midst. To counteract the structural shortcomings of national churches requires the entire church, able and willing even to proclaim some witnesses and martyrs as a means of fraternal correction of local churches.

If Jägerstätter speaks to the need of a wider community of reception, if Christian witness is to be accepted and made part of the life of the church, those converts to Catholicism who were instrumental in reversing centuries of anti-Jewish hostility speak to another imperative—that of "converting the baptized," in the words of the Jesuit William O'Malley.[31] Oesterreicher, Thieme, Gurian, Baum, von Hildebrand, Fuchs, Zacharias, and more—all of them confronted a church so thoroughly accommodated to its surrounding culture that the church itself disappeared in crucial ways.

In some respects, this is a more difficult matter than finding ways that Catholic transnational ties might counteract the pathologies of Catholic nationalism as a barrier to witness and prophetic reception. But this second lesson is no less crucial: for there to be Christian witness and reception, there has to be—at some significant level of thought and practice—a meaningful distinction between church and world, between the people gathered by God to reflect however imperfectly the dawning kingdom of God and those parts of reality still tied to other ambitions, other allegiances, and other loyalties.

This is a hard word for many Christians, especially many Catholics, to hear. We are so deeply steeped in those laudable parts of our tradition that stress the continuities between faith and reason, between the work of the Holy Spirit inside and outside the walls of the church, and the capacity of the gospel to become inculturated in all human communities and traditions, and are so deeply formed by these notions that we too often lose sight of the peculiarity of Christian testimony and the strangeness of Christian witness. If there is no disjunction of any sort between the church and the world, then there is no good news to proclaim, there is no need for a people capable of

---

31. William O'Malley, *Converting the Baptized: A Survival Manual for Parents, Teachers, and Pastors* (Allen, TX: Tabor Publishing, 1990).

trying to love their enemies, turning the other cheek, or repaying evil with good; the world does not need followers of Jesus if church and world are indistinguishable, saying and wanting the same things just with different terms or jargon.

The Jewish converts to Christianity who are so central to Connelly's account reminded the later church, at some level, of the irretrievably "other-ness" of the Christian faith—that this received final vindication during the Second Vatican Council, which affirmed the commonalities between church and world in many respects, is no small irony. And yet, perhaps this is not so surprising: persons witnessing to a new view of Judaism in Catholic circles did so not in response to Kantian ideals or generic ethical systems but by recourse to resources and readings and spiritual traditions out of step with the modern world of European scholarship. *Nouvelle théologie*, with its return to patristic sources and theological readings of Scripture, was out of touch not only with Catholic Neoscholasticism but also with secular modernity and its categories.

What the converts brought to the process, among other things, was a deep and profound encounter with the Jesus of the New Testament—in all his particularity and strangeness. This encounter pushed them beyond the natural law, universal morality, common grace, and secular notions of ethics and equality; in doing so, they sought to revitalize the spiritual taste buds, theological imaginations, and corporate practices of their Catholic brothers and sisters who had previously been more deeply formed by worldly stories and identities in which the distinctions between church and world were obscured—and thereby rendering them numb or immune to the call of the gospel as it related to the Jews.

It is this specificity, this insistence that the church and the world are not yet the same, that makes witness and its reception a radically Christocentric enterprise, and that makes the centrality of the poor in Christian life and reflection something other than nonsensical. Christian formation that loses this part of the dialectic—that stresses the continuities between God's creation and the ubiquity of the Holy Spirit at the expense of the utter otherness of Jesus Christ as the template for Christian discipleship, witness, and reception—finds itself with nothing to say and no ability to hear, rendered mute and deaf in varying measures.

3

Witnesses as Theological Sources*

Todd Walatka

As this volume of essays attests, the categories of "testimony" and "witness" are rich and multifaceted. To witness is a task to which each Christian and the whole church are called. Yet, as Michael Budde suggests,[1] it is imperative to reflect on the necessity and process of the *reception* of witnessing. If saintly witness is to bear fruit in our world, it must eventually fall upon fertile soil that welcomes and nourishes it as part of communal remembrance. Too often, witnesses to the truth are seen as overly radical, and thus their truth falls on rocky ground, starving the world of the fruit of such a life; or perhaps more often, the truth of witnesses is actively suppressed by an entrenched status quo, choking off the new possibilities opened up by authentic witnesses to truth and life. For the witness to lead others to greater truth—of God, ourselves, sin, the world, and much else—his or her life must be received, affirmed, and proclaimed by the community that is nourished by that testimony and in which witnesses will endure.

In this essay I would like to reflect on the reception of saintly witness within the church, but more specifically within theology. Rather than simply providing edifying examples for the Christian life, I argue that these witnesses should impact both the way we perceive the revelation of God in the history of Israel and Jesus Christ and the way we understand the Christian life as a response to this revelation. The witness of the saints should be understood as *sources* for theological reflection, not only for Christian ethics, but also for more traditional "dogmatic" topics such as Christology. In what follows I

---

* I would like to thank Gerald McKenny, Cyril O'Regan, Jennifer Martin, and Brian Hamilton for their helpful comments at various points in the development of this essay.

1. See the essay by Michael Lee in this volume.

sketch a framework for thinking about the place of witnesses within theology. This framework is structured by three primary goods, each drawn from a distinctive theological voice: namely, from Karl Barth, Hans Urs von Balthasar, and Jon Sobrino.[2] I start with Karl Barth's insistence on the *preeminence of witness* as a category for structuring the Christian life. In the final volumes of *Church Dogmatics*, Barth sees the task of witnessing as the most defining quality of the Christian life; he resists, however, a call to turn to successful Christian witnesses as theological sources. After exploring this resistance, I turn to Hans Urs von Balthasar's theology of sanctity and, in particular, Balthasar's vision of *the iconicity of the saint*. Balthasar shares Barth's concerns regarding human goods measuring divine goods, but insists that the lives and words of the saints are able to mediate the truth and beauty of revelation in a stable-enough way that they can become fruitful theological sources. Finally, I turn to Jon Sobrino's account of the witness of the martyrs in El Salvador. Though he does not use this language, Sobrino shares in a certain way Balthasar's view of the saint as an icon of Christ, but insists on the inherent *political character of all witnessing* and, in particular, the necessity of the option for the poor in Christian witness. In this essay I draw out these three goods, but with two corrective transitions that enable a fuller account of the place of witnesses within theology. Iconicity is precisely what is lacking in Barth; a robust account of political witness and the preferential option is what is deficient in Balthasar.

Karl Barth: Witness as the Center of Christian Existence

Karl Barth, perhaps more than any other theologian, places the task of witnessing at the center of the Christian life. In this section I detail his understanding of Christian witness, his fundamental theological commitments that shape this understanding, and then finally his resistance to the appeal to witnesses as actual theological sources.

---

2. It should be clear from the beginning that I do not seek a pure synthesis of what Barth, von Balthasar, and Sobrino think about witnessing; though they share key similarities, each structures the Christian faith according to his own logic, and at certain points, their positions remain incompatible. Instead, I draw upon one central aspect of each in order to construct a framework for thinking about witnesses in theology.

Near the end of his *Church Dogmatics*, Barth entertains a number of competing possibilities for what could be *the* defining aspect of Christian existence, for what distinguishes the Christian from all others: for example, a genuine life of freedom in the world; or a distinctive and compelling vision for human life and ethical conduct; or even the enjoyment of the benefits of the salvation won by Christ.[3] Barth clearly recognizes the deep existential impact of God's calling and grace on the life of the Christian, but he warns of the temptation to make what benefits *me* the essence and central goal of the Christian life.[4] In contrast, he argues that it is God's calling in vocation that marks the Christian, and this calling always propels one outward with a particular task, which is to *witness*. All the other benefits and gifts given to followers of Christ are in service of this task:

> The essence of their vocation is that God makes them His witnesses . . . he makes them witnesses of His being in His past, present, and future action in the world and in history, of His being in His acts among and upon men . . . this is what makes them what they are in distinction from all others. Whatever else they may be, and especially their being, capacity and possession graciously granted as their particular experience of salvation, the ethos especially required of them, and all that they might have to undergo in the way of particular suffering—all this depends upon and stands under the common sign of the fact that they are entrusted with this declaration and message and have to discharge this commission. They are witnesses. They are *Verbi divini ministri*.[5]

This calling to witness is the fundamental *ratio* of the Christian life, and it is the task of *all* Christians. In witnessing, the Christian freely cooperates in the prophetic work of Christ as a herald of Christ's person and work.[6] Ultimately, it is *Christ* who witnesses as *Word* to his

---

3. Karl Barth, *Church Dogmatics*, ed. G. W. Bromiley and T. F. Torrance; trans. G. W. Bromiley (Edinburgh: T. & T. Clark, 1957-1975), IV/3, 558-61.

4. See ibid., 563, 567. In short, one must focus not on the gifts but on the giver (596)

5. Ibid., 575-76.

6. For a clear summary of this prophetic work, see ibid., 606. See also IV/3, 599-600, IV/2, 592, and Colin Gunton, *The Barth Lectures* (London: T. & T. Clark, 2007), 228-30.

own work, but the Christian has the responsibility and task to act as a "cooperating assistant" in service to Christ,[7] summoned to attest to the victory of Christ and to the reality of the kingdom. The Christian is called on to confirm and glorify in one's life what is true in Christ.[8] This witness takes the form of, *inter alia*, proclamation, concrete love of neighbor, and willingness to suffer persecution in the world.

In order to further deepen Barth's understanding of witness, two of his core commitments need to be mentioned. The first is how radically and completely Barth locates the reality of reconciliation in Christ.[9] In contrast to Christ's prophetic work, the priestly and kingly works—bringing about justification and sanctification—are fully achieved in Christ with no cooperation on our part. Sanctification, as much as justification, is objectively real for all, but this is accomplished and made visible in Christ as representative rather than in his followers.[10] On the one hand, Barth does hold that real, subjectively experienced transformation is possible and indeed necessary for witnessing. Personal experience never becomes the *content* of one's witness, but an inchoate experience of the radical liberation brought in Christ is a presupposi-

---

7. The priority of Christ in his prophetic work is clear throughout Barth's treatment: "He alone is competent and authorized to perform it. He alone is the Speaker of the Word of God as well as the Doer of His work. . . . But in exercise of this prophetic office of His, even though it is He alone who controls it, He does not will to be alone. Controlling and exercising it, He calls certain men to His side and commissions them to be His disciples or pupils, i.e., Christians" (Barth, *Church Dogmatics,* IV/3, 606, 656). See also John Webster's comment on the simultaneous establishment and relativizing of the Christian in the task of witnessing in John Webster, *Karl Barth* (London and New York: Continuum, 2000), 136. In further describing our role, Barth says that "service" gets it just right: "Too much is not said, for the work is Christ's and he can only assist in total and not just partial subordination. Nor is too little, for as this co-operating assistant in the work of Christ he does acquire and take and have his own share, to be responsibly fulfilled" (*Church Dogmatics,* IV/3, 602). Our role—as individuals and as a church (803)—is not indispensable (607), and yet is it is real cooperation in the work of proclaiming Christ and the kingdom.

8. See Barth, *Church Dogmatics* IV/2, 544, and Gerald McKenny, *The Analogy of Grace: Karl Barth's Moral Theology* (New York: Oxford University Press, 2010), 70, 140-41.

9. See Joseph Mangina, *Karl Barth: Theologian of Christian Witness* (Louisville: Westminster, 2004), 119.

10. Barth, *Church Dogmatics,* IV/2, 511-33.

tion for witnessing well.[11] On the other hand, Barth's emphasis remains elsewhere; although human conduct is to confirm and actualize subjectively what is true objectively in Christ, Barth's account of sanctification "is still determined by [a] distinction between a perceptible self as sinner and an imperceptible self as righteous."[12]

The second commitment is the basic structure of Barth's theology of the Word. In witnessing, human beings share in Christ's prophetic work of proclaiming the truth of his person and work. As mentioned above, although this service can rightfully be called cooperation, it is ultimately the self-witness of the Word of God that makes our witness effective. Furthermore, despite the occasional use of visual images, aural analogies dominate Barth's account—accentuating the "event" character of the witness. To be a witness is to be a *speaker* rather than an *image* of the Word. Barth is clear that the Word is *always* mediated to us in some human form. Significantly, he does not exclude non-Christian and secular realities as possible witnesses.[13] Yet, witnesses in the church and world are only "indirect witnesses," whose lights shine only in the moment when the Word's light shines through them. Thus, no attempt can be made to synthesize these smaller words with the One Word.[14] The witness does not become a stable reality that sheds light on Christ. What makes a witness effective is not a certain movement from sinfulness to holiness or conformity to God's life and will; rather, it is the decision of the Word to speak.

These two fundamental presuppositions govern Barth's understanding of witnessing throughout the entirety of his *Church Dogmatics*, but one also finds a subtle shift in language. In earlier parts Barth occasionally uses sacramental language;[15] he suggests that a line

---

11. Barth, *Church Dogmatics,* IV/3, 676.

12. McKenny, *The Analogy of Grace,* 67. McKenny further explains, "While the theology of the command of God makes it possible to understand the sanctification of concrete human conduct . . . sanctification remains an eschatological (while at the same time a Christological) reality."

13. See his discussion of "secular parables of the Kingdom," in *Church Dogmatics,* IV/3, 112-35. See also Kenneth Oakes, *Karl Barth on Theology & Philosophy* (Oxford: Oxford University Press, 2012), 255.

14. Barth, *Church Dogmatics,* IV/3, 96, 101.

15. This is particularly true in his discussion of love of neighbor in Barth, *Church Dogmatics,* I/2, 401-54, interestingly placed under the title of "The Praise of God."

of witnesses from the Christ-event forms a "sacramental continuity," representing it to new ages.[16] In this light he will speak of Jesus Christ "present to us" in "good neighbors," who are in some way "bearer[s] and representative[s] of the mercy of God."[17] He speaks in a similar way regarding those who are poor and afflicted.[18] Given that one witnesses with one's life and not just words, by definition Barth will always affirm that there must be a real correspondence between the transformed life and good works and God's gracious action on behalf of humanity. Nevertheless, even as this affirmation of correspondence remains,[19] later parts of the *Church Dogmatics* tend to downplay the perspicuity of the witness in revealing Christ; the reflection will always be "provisional" and "quite inadequate. It can never be more than a replica which indicates and suggests the original only very distantly and indistinctly."[20] This is true for three reasons. First, Barth continually insists that we must resist the temptation to identify what other human beings do too closely with what God has graciously done for us in Christ.[21] Second, our sinfulness distorts our becoming a fitting human analogue to the truth found in Christ. Finally, in light of Barth's theology of the Word, there is always an inherent instability to the witness in its dependence on God's accompanying action in a particular moment. Barth describes the Christian as a rock-face who in no sense can produce an echo, as a reflector with no intrinsic power

---

16. Barth, *Church Dogmatics,* II/1, 54; quoted in Mangina, *Karl Barth,* 61.

17. Barth, *Church Dogmatics,* I/2, 424, 421.

18. "The afflicted fellow-man is actually the representative of Jesus Christ. As such he is actually the bearer and representative of divine compassion. As such he actually directs us to the right praise of God" (Barth, *Church Dogmatics,* I/2, 429). In these examples Barth is reflecting upon the story of the Good Samaritan in Luke 10 and the parable of the last judgment in Matthew 25.

19. For example, the Christian is called to never "cease to be that little light reflecting the great light" (Barth, *Church Dogmatics,* IV/1, 778; see 775-76 as well).

20. Barth, *Church Dogmatics,* IV/3, 674.

21. This point was illustrated above in the discussion of Christ's priestly and kingly work. For Barth, Christ has already done everything to constitute our relation to God in grace. The Christian must not seek to do what only Christ can do (and *has done*), and lifting up certain witnesses for emulation or as theological sources can obscure this basic distinction between Christ's salvific work and our living in light of that work. I am grateful to Gerald McKenny for comments on this concern of Barth.

of illumination: "it is the voice of Jesus which brings sound from the rock-face and His light which brings light from the reflector."[22] Barth thus resists any attempt to lift up certain Christian lives as monuments or to look to them in order to see revelation more clearly. We do not examine the rock-face in order to learn more about the initial Word; we simply respond to the Word heard in the echo off the rock.

To sum up, Barth strongly insists that the central purpose of the Christian life is to witness to Christ's victory over the powers of the world. This task of witness is to structure all other aspects of the Christian life. In the end, however, witnesses are not epistemologically significant for the theological task. In general, Barth is intensely worried about human realities being lifted up as equals to or in competition with Christ.[23] Then these may become a measure of Christ rather than being measured by him. Furthermore, as we have seen, the correspondence to Christ necessary for witnessing is neither pure enough nor stable enough for the witnesses to be given a place in theological reflection. One may hear God's call in the witness of others, and in this case one must respond; but it is not the norm to turn to these witnesses as a means for illuminating God's revelation in Christ. For this move we must turn to von Balthasar.

Hans Urs von Balthasar: The Saints as Theological Resources

Balthasar, of course, was heavily influenced by Barth, and in particular by the Christocentric (and trinitarian) shape of the latter's theology. This Christocentrism is important for understanding Balthasar, and yet, as I will detail below, it is Balthasar's accompanying *pneumatology* that provides a place for saintly witnesses within the theological task.

Following Barth, Balthasar places the mission of the Son at the center of all of history. In dramatic terms, Jesus is the protagonist who, under the guidance of the Holy Spirit (the director), freely, creatively, and obediently performs the playwright's intention to bring salvation to the world.[24] At the center of the drama, Balthasar sees

---

22. Barth, *Church Dogmatics,* IV/3, 614.

23. This is the point that is most apparent in his critique of Balthasar in *Church Dogmatics,* IV/1, 768.

24. Hans Urs von Balthasar, *Theo-Drama: Theological Dramatic Theory,*

Jesus as a vertical irruption into horizontal history, and everything either points to or flows from this center and cannot be evaluated in isolation from it.[25] He even goes so far as to say that all that is left from a *theological* point of view are the interpretation and continuing effects of this event.[26] Balthasar also fully agrees with Barth that saintly witnesses must not direct one away from God's revelation in Christ; this is particularly clear in Balthasar's continual concern that spirituality and ideals of holiness sometimes focus too much on the inner workings of human experience rather than the conformation of the person to Christ.[27] Nevertheless, a recurring theme in Balthasar's theodramatics shows their divergence: Christ's mission is inclusive. One of the "continuing effects" of the Christ-event is the very drawing of humanity into the salvific action, bringing us into Jesus' mission of reconciling the world to God. Not as mere rock-faces, human persons become *actors* in the drama and are called to "cooperate responsibly with God."[28]

Just as the concept of mission stands at the center of Balthasar's theodramatic Christology, it is likewise the core of his anthropology; and it is in the form of mission that Balthasar understands Christian witness. Witness is offered by responding to the call of God, propelled into the world with a task that is part of God's plan for the world. It is also in the sense of inclusion in Christ's all-embracing mission

---

Volume I: Prolegomena, trans. Graham Harrison (San Francisco: Ignatius, 1988), 259-305; cf. Aidan Nichols, O.P., *No Bloodless Myth: A Guide through Balthasar's Dramatics* (Washington, DC: Catholic University of America Press, 2000), 29-32; and Edward T. Oakes, *Pattern of Redemption: The Theology of Hans Urs von Balthasar* (New York: Continuum, 1994), 217-19.

25. Hans Urs von Balthasar, *Theo-Drama: Theological Dramatic Theory, Volume IV: The Action,* trans. Graham Harrison (San Francisco: Ignatius, 1994), 205-6.

26. Hans Urs von Balthasar, *Theo-Drama: Theological Dramatic Theory, Volume V: The Final Act,* trans. Graham Harrison (San Francisco: Ignatius, 1998), 49.

27. For one example, see Hans Urs von Balthasar, "Theology and Sanctity," in *Explorations in Theology I: The Word Made Flesh* (San Francisco: Ignatius, 1989), 181-209, at 191.

28. Balthasar, *Theo-Drama I,* 34; cf., Hans Urs Von Balthasar, *The Christian State of Life,* trans. Sister Mary Frances McCarthy (San Francisco: Ignatius, 1983), 401.

that Balthasar sees grace perfecting nature, the universal call to holiness, and the process of divinization. The Christian is the one who has given his or her existence up to Christ and "receives it back in the form of [a] mission and task for God's Kingdom in this world."[29]

For Balthasar, the *saints* are identified primarily as those witnesses who listen patiently and humbly for the call of God and obediently follow God's will in mission. Key to remember here is that these lives are part of Christ's all-embracing mission. Thus, through their holiness in living out their personal mission in Christ, saints reveal for the church something about this all-embracing mission. Balthasar suggests that if we want to understand who Jesus is, what he did, and what he experienced, we can turn to those who have lived holy lives and responded to God's call to carry out their mission in Christ. In this light, for Balthasar, saints are like *icons* of Christ, whose lives represent and draw us into the truth and beauty of God; beyond the surface, there is a Christological depth to the life of the saint that indicates something of God's mercy, judgment, and, ultimately, love of the world. In short, the saint is the one whose holy life is transparent to Christ in such a way that the truth of Christ shines through for the edification and salvation of others: "for the saints are not given to us to admire for their heroic powers, but that we should be enlightened by them on the inner reality of Christ, both for our better understanding of the faith and for our living thereby in charity."[30]

Balthasar is clear that there is a danger in focusing on the saints instead of Christ.[31] He is likewise clear that the lives of the saints—as they are still marked by sin—can obscure as well as illuminate.[32] Yet, Balthasar argues that pneumatology demands theological atten-

---

29. Hans Urs von Balthasar, *A Theology of History* (San Francisco: Ignatius, 1994), 119.

30. Balthasar, "Theology and Sanctity," 204. See also Hans Urs von Balthasar, *The Glory of the Lord: A Theological Aesthetics, Volume I: Seeing the Form*, trans. Erasmo Leiva-Merikakis (San Francisco: Ignatius, 1981), 28, and Danielle Nussberger, "Saint as Theological Wellspring: Hans Urs von Balthasar's Hermeneutic of the Saint in a Christological and Trinitarian Key" (Ph.D. diss., University of Notre Dame, 2007).

31. Balthasar, "Theology and Sanctity," 217.

32. See Hans Urs von Balthasar, *Two Sisters in the Spirit: Therese of Lisieux & Elizabeth of the Trinity*, trans. Donald Nichols, Anne Englund Nash, and Dennis Martin (San Francisco: Ignatius, 1992), 30-31.

tiveness to the saints. Jesus Christ is God's final and complete Word to humanity, but since this Word is spoken out of the unfathomable depths of God, greater understanding must continually be sought. And it is precisely the Holy Spirit that "will guide you into all truth" (John 16:13). For Balthasar, the Spirit witnesses to the truth of Christ and makes that truth alive in the world:

> It will be impossible to come to an end in declaring this truth all down through the ages . . . new vistas are continually being opened up on the infinite whole . . . sometimes, if the Spirit wills, we can suddenly become aware of entirely new aspects of the infinite truth as they come under the spotlight, aspects that always had their place within the faith's spiritual horizon but were somehow neglected. The oft-repeated dictum is true: There is much more truth in Christ than the Church's faith and much more truth in the Church's faith than in the formulated dogmas. People with great charisms, like Augustine, Francis, and Ignatius, can be granted (by the Spirit) glimpses of the very center of revelation, and these glimpses can enrich the Church in the most unexpected and yet permanent way. Insight, love, and discipleship are always inseparable in such charisms, which show us that the Spirit who declares the truth is at the same time divine Love and divine Wisdom: he is by no means mere theory, but the inspirer of a lived life.[33]

Balthasar recognizes that the Spirit leads us to truth in many ways, including the inspired Scriptures, the development of dogma, and liturgical and sacramental traditions. Yet, his emphasis often lies on the saintly life as a means by which the Spirit illuminates some aspect of the truth that has remained unnoticed or ignored.[34] This is one of the main places where Balthasar's theological method becomes "correlational," shaped "from below" by human experience. Building upon this, Balthasar contends that God's primary response to urgent contemporary problems will come through saintly lives, which are "like volcanoes pouring forth molten fire from the inmost depths of

---

33. Hans Urs von Balthasar, *Theo-Logic, Volume III: The Spirit of Truth*, trans. Graham Harrison (San Francisco: Ignatius, 2005), 21.

34. See Balthasar, *Theo-Logic III*, 307-411, for Balthasar's extensive account of the "objective" and "subjective" sides of the Spirit's work.

revelation."[35] He suggests that the interpretation of revelation in any time must be done in the company of the saints:

> For the faithful, they are above all, a new type of conformity to Christ inspired by the Holy Spirit and therefore a new illustration of how the gospel is to be lived. For theologians, on the other hand, they are rather a new interpretation of revelation; they bring out the scarcely suspected treasures in the deposit of faith.[36]

Balthasar thus provides the second part of the framework for the role of witnesses within theology: iconicity. By the work of the Holy Spirit, the image, beauty, truth, and goodness of Christ are seen in saintly witnesses in such a way that the revelation of God in Christ is illuminated for the good of the church. As icons of Christ, saintly witnesses represent essential resources for reflecting on the person and work of Christ and the Christian life today. There is also, however, a certain narrowness in Balthasar's actual use of the saints. He focuses intensely on the prayerful receptivity to God's will that is the cornerstone of any saintly life. This is genuinely helpful and necessary. Equally helpful is Balthasar's insistence that holiness must not be reduced to one form of life, whether more nearly contemplative or outwardly activist in form.[37] Yet, Balthasar tends not to focus on the inevitable political side of any witness. Although it is possible to draw out political implications from Balthasar's use of St. Therese and to look at his lifting up of Reinhold Schneider's resistance in Nazi Germany,[38] even these will not take us far enough. A greater attentiveness to concrete social, political, and economic realities is needed.

---

35. Balthasar, *A Theology of History*, 109-10.

36. Balthasar, *Two Sisters in the Spirit*, 25; cf, Hans Urs von Balthasar, *Theo-Drama: Theological Dramatic Theory, Volume II: The Dramatis Personae: Man in God*, trans. Graham Harrison (San Francisco: Ignatius, 1990), 14.

37. See Balthasar, *A Theology of History*, 126; *Theo-drama I*, 126. As is clear from his idea of mission (and as a good follower of Ignatius of Loyola), Balthasar argues that contemplation and action must be intimately united in every Christian life, even if the outward form of life often tends toward one or the other.

38. Hans Urs von Balthasar, *Tragedy under Grace: Reinhold Schneider on the Experience of the West*, trans. Brian McNeil, C.R.V. (San Francisco: Ignatius, 1997).

In a world shaped by inequality and oppression, we need to turn to saintly witnesses, who unveil the sin of the world, illuminate God's love of the poor revealed in Scripture, and call for a new way of life.

Jon Sobrino and the Witnesses of El Salvador

Much of Sobrino's project could be seen as a prophetic call to ensure that the one whom we follow in faith is actually Jesus of Nazareth. An orthodox confession of Jesus as fully human and fully divine does not necessarily mean that a Christology is sufficiently grounded in the concrete particularity of Jesus and his praxis on behalf of the kingdom. To borrow familiar Balthasarian terminology, one's faith may be insufficiently aesthetic as it does not display the proper receptive disposition toward what has been revealed in Christ. Instead one ideologically makes of Christ what one wills. The danger here is captured well in the opening of Sobrino's *Jesus the Liberator:* "Let us remember that this continent has been subjected to centuries of inhuman and anti-Christian oppression, without christology giving any sign of having noticed this and certainly without it providing any prophetic denunciation in the name of Jesus Christ."[39] For Sobrino, certain witnesses can aid us overcoming this very real danger.

The witnesses to which Sobrino turns are the martyrs of El Salvador: Archbishop Romero, Sobrino's Jesuit brothers, and countless other men and women. For Sobrino, these witnesses to the kingdom in El Salvador have a key role in preserving the life-giving character of the gospel. Given that every interpretation and living out of the gospel is partially political in character, these martyrs witness to the need to make this dimension clear and to shape it with the option for the poor. The image Sobrino frequently uses when discussing the role of the martyrs is that of *shedding light.*[40] The martyrs shed light on the life of Christ, on the reality of the world, and on how to live the Christian life. In this way, they assume, perhaps with greater force, the same methodological place as the saints for Balthasar. In

---

39. Jon Sobrino, *Jesus the Liberator: A Historical-Theological Reading of Jesus of Nazareth*, trans. Paul Burns and Francis McDonagh (Maryknoll, NY: Orbis Books, 1994), 3.

40. See, for example, Jon Sobrino, *Witnesses to the Kingdom: The Martyrs of El Salvador and the Crucified Peoples* (Maryknoll NY: Orbis Books, 2003), 129.

this respect, Sobrino introduces the idea of the martyrs offering us a "witness Christology" as a complement to the text Christology of the Bible and Tradition.[41] This witness Christology helps us avoid overly abstract visions of Jesus, as Jesus' truth and message are re-presented in the historical flesh of the martyrs. In what follows I will provide three ways in which the martyrs offer this Christological complement in Sobrino's work.

First, Sobrino worries that visions of Jesus as good news are often truncated; in confessing Jesus as God and man, even as savior and liberator, his concrete manner of being, particularly his closeness and tenderness toward the weak, can be problematically downplayed.[42] Here Sobrino appeals to Romero and other witnesses as an aid for seeing the fullness of Jesus as good news. Romero's words and reflections on Christ certainly point in the right direction, but even more so it is Romero's own closeness to the poor and oppressed that resembles and thus draws our attention to this aspect of Christ.

Second, Sobrino argues that mercy for the suffering and vulnerable is at the core of Jesus' praxis: it is this reaction to the suffering of others that shapes his mission and ultimately seals his fate.[43] Mercy is commanded of the church and every Christian, and it is the reality that shaped the lives of the martyrs as well. According to Sobrino, "the most decisive part is knowing why [the martyrs] dedicated their lives to healing the wounded. The answer is extremely simple . . . in the presence of a crucified people, their hearts were moved and they were moved to mercy. They internalized the suffering of an entire people and responded to it."[44] In their mercy toward the poor—a mercy that leads to their deaths—these martyrs are icons of Christ; their mercy illuminates and draws our gaze to the mercy of Christ.

Third, the martyrs also shine a light on a world that resists the kingdom that Jesus proclaimed. In doing this, they also challenge others to be honest with reality and confront the forces of the anti-kingdom.

---

41. Jon Sobrino, *No Salvation outside the Poor: Prophetic–Utopian Essays* (Maryknoll, NY: Orbis Books, 2008), 109.

42. Jon Sobrino, *Christ the Liberator: A View from the Victims*, trans. Paul Burns (Maryknoll, NY: Orbis Books, 2001), 214.

43. Jon Sobrino, *The Principle of Mercy: Taking the Crucified People from the Cross* (Maryknoll, NY: Orbis Books, 1994), 17.

44. Ibid., 175.

At the most basic level, the death of the martyrs forces people *to pay attention*: Sobrino writes, "People finally had to look Salvadoran reality in the eye. 'Something is very wrong in El Salvador,' our martyrs cried."[45] These martyrs shine a light on the falsehood and deception of those who want to maintain an oppressive status quo; in this way they also guide the way forward for followers of Christ today.

In all three of these points Sobrino draws out aspects of Christian witness that are necessary in a world marked by oppression. In a world of great inequality and structures of sin, there is no such thing as an apolitical life or witness. All witnesses are political, at least in the sense of their concrete ramifications in the political realm. The martyrs of El Salvador are icons of the preferential option; their witness points to the preferential option made by God in Christ and to its essential role in the lives of those who follow him.

A Brief Conclusion

In this essay I have provided a framework for thinking about the *reception* of saintly witnesses within the work of theology by tracing the idea of witness through Barth, Balthasar, and Sobrino and drawing together commitments to the preeminence of witness, the iconicity of the saint, and the political character of all witnesses. In the end, the framework I propose remains largely within the conceptual space of Balthasar; however, it also incorporates key aspects of Barth and is particularly challenged and shaped by Sobrino's meditations on the martyrs of El Salvador.

In final analysis, it is Balthasar's sacramental pneumatology that enables the witness to play such a significant role in illuminating revelation and the Christian life. Although Balthasar is rightly seen as a Christocentric thinker, it is the role of the Holy Spirit in drawing others into the mission of Christ that provides a strong theological foundation for thinking about witness. In a particularly striking passage, given what we saw in Sobrino, Balthasar argues that

> Without [the Holy Spirit], the picture our spirit makes of Jesus is pale and flat, unable to embrace the tensions in which Jesus reveals the unity of God's innermost mind. This is sufficiently

---

45. Sobrino, *The Principle of Mercy*, 183.

proved by the innumerable pictures of Jesus which people have drawn after their own liking, pictures of a mild, basically dull Savior whose "solidarity" with the poor, oppressed and sinners no longer glows red hot, where nothing really divine shines through.[46]

It is ultimately the Holy Spirit who keeps alive the truth of Christ in the church and the world down through the centuries. This work of the Spirit is accomplished particularly in the saintly witnesses and martyrs who play their role well in the drama of salvation. In the martyrs of El Salvador we see the love and solidarity of Jesus glowing red hot; we see the love and will of God shining through. In their service to and speaking out for the poor, the witness of the martyrs of El Salvador can be seen as one of the ways in which the Holy Spirit is speaking to our age.

---

46. Hans Urs von Balthasar, *Does Jesus Know Us? Do We Know Him?*, trans. Graham Harrison (San Francisco: Ignatius, 1983), 86.

4

Hearing the Cries of Crucified Peoples: The Prayerful Witness of Ignacio Ellacuría and James Cone

Andrew Prevot

Testimony can be defined as a self-implicating disclosure of the truth. This definition is connected with the ordinary realm of judicial proceedings, in which witnesses are asked to report on the facts of a situation and to stake their reputation and potentially their freedom on their sworn statements. It is linked to the interpretive practice of "attestation," which is central to Paul Ricoeur's influential account of the nonfoundational subject of hermeneutical phenomenology. It applies to the act of "testifying," common in many "free church" worship services, in which members of the community recount their conversion experiences and spiritual journeys in order to edify the gathered assembly. And, finally, it takes on a particularly intense form in the bloody history of Christian martyrdom, which runs from the earliest years of the Christian tradition up to the present day. This history includes the many Christlike witnesses of the twentieth century who suffered and died defending the truth of the gospel in El Salvador and in the civil rights and black power movements of the United States. From this short list of examples, it becomes clear that testimony, the self-implicating disclosure of the truth, can take shape in many different ways. Even the specifically Christian sense of the term allows for a variety of interpretations.[1]

---

1. See Paul Ricoeur, *Oneself as Another*, trans. Kathleen Blamey (Chicago: University of Chicago Press, 1992), 21-23; Rosetta Ross, *Witnessing and Testifying: Black Women, Religion, and Civil Rights* (Minneapolis: Augsburg Fortress Press, 2003), 13-14; Candida Moss, *Ancient Christian Martyrdom: Diverse Practices,*

In this essay, I shall reflect on two such interpretations, as provided by the Jesuit, Latin American liberation theologian Ignacio Ellacuría and the U.S. black liberation theologian James Cone. In particular, I shall argue that the specific kinds of testimony that figure prominently in their writings and their lives emerge from a Christian experience of *prayer*, that is (to speak rather generally at the moment) a dialogue between divine and human freedom that takes place in and through Christ and the Holy Spirit. Both Ellacuría and Cone deepen the meaning of prayer through distinct prayerful traditions, as we shall see below. Moreover, they associate prayer not only with solitary or communal practices of devotion but also with physically costly acts of public struggle performed for the sake of, and in solidarity with, the victims of history. Prayer thus becomes for them the font of an entire way of life, or *spirituality*, in which dialogical communion with God (*orare*) flows into and provides an abiding interpretive context for liberative work (*laborare*) in the world.[2] Christian testimony is achieved through the organic unity of these two. The truth that sets us free (John 8:32) and the selves that are responsible for the communication of this truth originate in prayer; they are inconceivable without it. At the same time, the worldly labor that discloses this truth in the light of day and implicates prayerful selves in life-or-death battles for its greater realization demonstrates the full corporeal weight of prayer (its "price") and confirms the testimonial significance of Christian spirituality as a whole.

It may be helpful to look more closely at what is at stake in each side of this indivisible whole. According to Ellacuría and Cone, any Christian spirituality that bears witness to the liberating truth of the gospel must include social, economic, and political analyses and practices that promote the work of liberation in every concrete sphere

---

Theologies, and Traditions (New Haven: Yale University Press, 2012), 2-7; Jon Sobrino and Ignacio Ellacuría et al., *Companions of Jesus: The Jesuit Martyrs of El Salvador* (Maryknoll, NY: Orbis Books, 1990); and James Cone, *Martin & Malcolm & America: A Dream or a Nightmare* (Maryknoll, NY: Orbis Books, 1991).

2. The close connection between *orare* and *laborare* has been highlighted especially by the Benedictine tradition of Christian monasticism. Ellacuría and Cone take this connection in a more "apostolic" direction, integrating it with the needs and struggles of the victims of history.

of human existence. Through these critical measures, Ellacuría and Cone encourage a way of life that is able to develop and enact realistic strategies for taking the "crucified peoples" down from their crosses.[3] They surmise, quite reasonably, that such a liberative spirituality cannot be confined to the quiet times that we spend alone with God, even if these times become genuinely solidaristic through the mysterious powers of empathy and intercession that operate through prayer. On the contrary, a truly testimonial spirituality of Christian freedom must courageously come forth into the world and there take its stand, even if this means (at it often does) imperiling the lives of those who profess it.[4]

Without in any way diluting this action-oriented message, both Ellacuría and Cone affirm that prayer is essential to such a testimonial spirituality. They see prayer as the permanent, illuminating, and empowering source of any Christian witness that desires to be deeply receptive to the liberating power of God. True Christian prayer understands and teaches, as nothing else can, that unjust structures of oppressive violence are a grave offense against God insofar as they defile God's own beloved creatures and, moreover, that these same structures are susceptible to the promised victory of God's infinite justice and love, which already comes to us in Christ and the Spirit. In the midst of their respective liberation struggles, Ellacuría and Cone never forget this insight. They never forget the radically transformative relationship of divine and human freedom that prayer brings to life, a relationship that is found not only in explicit acts of prayer (supplication, meditation, song, and so on) but also in sustained prayerful dispositions conducive to a habit of prayer without ceasing (1 Thes-

---

3. In Ellacuría's foundational essay "The Crucified People," in *Mysterium Liberationis: Fundamental Concepts of Liberation Theology*, ed. Ignacio Ellacuría and Jon Sobrino (Maryknoll, NY: Orbis Books, 1993), 580-603, he does not speak of taking the crucified people down from their crosses but rather of seeking their historical resurrection (603). The clearest expression of the former idea comes in Sobrino's *The Principle of Mercy: Taking the Crucified People Down from the Cross* (Maryknoll, NY: Orbis Books, 1994), 55. See also Cone's citation of Sobrino in *The Cross and the Lynching Tree* (Maryknoll, NY: Orbis Books, 2011), 161.

4. See Ignacio Ellacuría, *Fe y justicia* (Bilbao, Spain: Editorial Desclée de Brouwer, 1999), 214, and James Cone, *God of the Oppressed* (Maryknoll, NY: Orbis Books, 2010), 34. Admittedly, Ellacuría and Cone do not concern themselves with offering sympathetic accounts of any "purely" contemplative vocations.

salonians 5:17), which remains foundational in Ellacuría's and Cone's proposed forms of liberating, innerworldly action. Indeed, the prayerful relationship of divine and human freedom is largely constitutive of the *definitively* liberating truth to which both Ellacuría and Cone believe all Christians are called to bear witness and, moreover, of the particular kinds of *theonomously* agentive selves that they suggest must be implicated in this witnessing. In short, Ellacuría and Cone offer an understanding of a liberative Christian testimony that, without departing from worldly struggle, is thoroughly infused by prayer.

Ellacuría's and Cone's agreement on these points indicates a profound unity of spiritual and theological vision, which has thus far received very little attention from their respective commentators.[5] I would like to begin filling this lacuna. However, I do not wish to suggest that their treatments of Christian testimony are the same in every relevant respect. Theirs remains a unity-in-diversity. The differences between Ellacuría and Cone are not reducible to the general distinction between anticapitalist and antiracist critique, which remains the most typical way of contrasting the broader movements of Latin American and black liberation theology to which these two theologians belong. I shall not dwell extensively on this distinction here, since it has been greatly complicated and even somewhat diminished in recent years by a growing awareness of intersecting oppressions. There is now an emerging consensus that we need to overcome the damaging effects of both maldistributed wealth and white-dominated culture.[6]

I shall focus more attention on other important differences related to the particular spiritual traditions that Ellacuría and Cone inhabit.

---

5. For example, one may note the lack of attention to this connection in Kevin Burke and Robert Lassalle-Klein, eds., *Love That Produces Hope: The Thought of Ignacio Ellacuría* (Collegeville, MN: Liturgical Press, 2006), and Dwight Hopkins, ed., *Black Faith and Public Talk: Critical Essays on James H. Cone's "Black Theology and Black Power"* (Maryknoll, NY: Orbis Books, 1999). This two-sided inattention is understandable, given the distance in context between these two theologians, but there is also something to be gained from overcoming it.

6. For Cone's account of the relationship between these movements, see his "From Geneva to São Paulo: A Dialogue between Black Theology and Latin American Liberation Theology," in *Black Theology: A Documentary History, Volume 2: 1980-1992*, ed. James Cone and Gayraud Wilmore (Maryknoll, NY: Orbis Books, 1993), 371-87.

Whereas Ellacuría's testimony takes shape through an innovative appropriation and "historicization" of Ignatius of Loyola's *Spiritual Exercises*, Cone's testimony grows out of his efforts to retrieve the theological and practical wisdom of the pre–Civil War black church, especially as this is expressed in the spirituals of the slaves. Each of these spiritual traditions is highly significant in its original historical context. They are doubly significant when reinterpreted amid the crises of the present age, and this is one way of understanding the theological achievements of both Ellacuría and Cone. Finally, these traditions are triply significant when brought together, as I hope to show here.

This third level of combined significance most obviously includes a unified contestation of both socio-economic and racial oppression, as well as a sense of ecumenical closeness between Protestant and Catholic, black and white, North and South, and past and present traditions—but this is not all. It also unites two complementary vocations of testimonial spirituality, which are not always sufficiently distinguished or balanced. On the one hand, there is a call to *kenosis* that leads the Christian who may initially be outside a situation of unjust suffering to risk entering more deeply into that situation in imitation of Christ, in accordance with the promptings of the Spirit, and in solidarity with the present-day crucified peoples. This is the primary movement we find in Ellacuría. On the other hand, there is a call to hope in the midst of unjust suffering, a call that gives consolation to the crucified peoples themselves, that reflects the active presence of Christ and the Spirit in their midst, and that can be found both in their precarious hymnody and in their ongoing historical struggles. This is the primary movement we find in Cone. Traces of each vocation are evident in both theologians; so dichotomous thinking should be avoided here. Nevertheless, there is a difference of emphasis that is noteworthy and fruitful. These two dimensions of testimonial spirituality can be brought together to form a more complete whole.

With Ellacuría and Cone, therefore, we have two very distinctive, relevant, and mutually enriching examples of the prayerful and liberating character of Christian witness. Together, these examples accomplish more than any account of testimony that would rely primarily on transcendental, ontological, or even abstractly ethical categories, as one finds in Martin Heidegger's philosophy and also, to some extent, in Emmanuel Levinas's and Paul Ricoeur's.[7] The finite exposition of being through the achievement of one's ownmost potentiality (Heidegger), the signification, through ethical substitution, of a generalized other (Levinas), and the moderate hermeneutical mediation of these two possibilities (Ricoeur) leave too much undecided. A much greater promise of freedom lies in a constitutively prayerful self that manifests the liberating presence of the triune God through solidaristic and hopeful actions in explicit resistance against the socioeconomically and racially violent structures of the modern world. To clarify the promise of such an adamantly and authentically Christian testimony, I shall discuss Ellacuría's and Cone's contributions in turn and then offer some concluding thoughts regarding the benefits that may come from synthesizing their positions.

The Testimony of Ignacio Ellacuría

One should not underestimate the profound influence that Archbishop Oscar Romero's martyrial witness had on Ellacuría's subsequent theological and practical reflections. Nor should one neglect the host of other formative teachers and mentors, such as Karl Rahner, Xavier Zubiri, Angel Martinez, and Miguel Elizondo, who likewise shaped Ellacuría's self-implicating efforts to disclose the liberating truth of the gospel amid the grave historical conditions of El Salvador in the 1960s, '70s, and '80s. Nevertheless, it seems appropriate to acknowledge a certain kind of priority in the influence of Ignatius, and particularly in Ignatius's way of encouraging retreatants to contemplate and imitate the example of Christ. This is a lesson that Ellacuría internalized very deeply through his spiritual practice as a Jesuit (from his novitiate onward) and that he, moreover, never ceased to express in his scholarly works.[8]

In a short text entitled "Lectura latinoamericana de los *Ejercicios*

---

7. For an overview of this philosophical tradition of testimony and its aporias, see Ricoeur, *Oneself as Another*, 297-356.

8. See Robert Lasalle-Klein, "Introduction," and J. Matthew Ashley, "Contemplation in the Action of Justice: Ignacio Ellacuría and Ignatian Spirituality," in *Love That Produces Hope*, xii-xxxv and 144-67. See also several of Ellacuría's essays in his *Escritos teológicos*, vol. 4 (San Salvador: UCA Editores, 2002), 47-122 and 173-289.

espirituales de san Ignacio," Ellacuría traces the basic features of Ignatian spirituality through each of the major parts of the *Spiritual Exercises*, emphasizing the need for Christians to model their own lives
on the totality of Christ's existence.[9] Ellacuría argues that an Ignatian
form of *imitatio Christi* involves a confrontation with sin that occurs
in the midst of the concrete realities of life, in expectation of death,
and in hope of resurrection. This is the structure that is illuminated
by the Four Weeks.[10] Moreover, Ellacuría clarifies that the purpose of
this confrontation is to "praise, reverence, and serve" the God of our
salvation and to cultivate a contemplative space in which the creature
can venture ever more deeply and freely into communion with the
creator's self-giving love. This, he says, is the message of the Principle
and Foundation and the Contemplation to Attain Love.[11]

Finally, Ellacuría contends that Ignatius's spirituality is fundamentally animated by a process of spiritual discernment through which
one not only meditates on the saving actions that God has already
revealed and accomplished in Christ but also makes concrete decisions about how best to reorient one's life in a Christic manner in the
midst of current historical circumstances (and he has in mind here
particularly the death-dealing poverty of the Third World). This is
the goal of the Election.[12] The resulting decision, following the dic-
tates of the Spirit of Christ, which moves freely in each individual's
heart, as well as in communal acts of discernment, will always be particular to one's own situation. At the same time, the true Spirit will
invariably draw one away from the worldly idols of "riches, honor,
and pride" and toward the loving *kenosis* of the Son, a contrast that is
depicted most clearly in the Meditation on the Two Standards.[13] Ellacuría concludes that embodying the fruits of this spiritual discernment in a simultaneously contemplative and active spirituality is the
primary way in which Jesus' followers can participate meaningfully in
God's ongoing work of salvation *in* history.[14] This is one of Ellacuría's

---

9. Ignacio Ellacuría, "Lectura latinoamericana de los *Ejercicios espirituales
de san Ignacio,"* in *Escritos teológicos,* vol. 4, 59-106.

10. Ibid., 69-99.

11. Ibid., 67-69, 100-102.

12. Ibid., 64, 81.

13. Ibid., 82-87.

14. Ibid., 106.

most important theological concepts, and we find it emerging here precisely from his spirituality.[15]

A few points should be made about the kind of testimony that is implicit in this account. First, one should note that the sort of truth that is disclosed in Ellacuría's elaboration of Ignatian spirituality is not primarily abstract or formal. It is not a truth focused on the most general categories of being, of transcendental consciousness, or even of sentient intelligence and sensible reality, as Zubiri understands these terms.[16] Rather, this is a truth that is thoroughly concretized by the interactions of divine and human freedom that have taken place in the troubled history of the created world and particularly in biblical revelation and the then-current reality of Latin America. The horizon of this truth is not ontology or indeterminate alterity but rather a living encounter with the Christologically revealed and pneumatologically efficacious presence of the saving God in history.

Despite his unmistakable reverence for divine love—and, indeed, precisely in order to understand its historical implications—Ellacuría insists that a conflict must occur with the deadly realities of sin that contradict this love. The truth is therefore not only that God loves us and that we are called to love in response (though obviously this is crucial) but also that this same love involves both God and humanity in a perilous fight against the many life-negating forces that dominate the fallen world. Ellacuría is concerned particularly with certain "alienating, unjust, and inhumane" societies that have been founded on the suffering of the impoverished masses.[17] The insufficiently liberated historical reality of such societies is a contrastive aspect of the liberating truth that must be disclosed in Christian testimony. To understand the freedom that God is working to bestow upon humanity, partly through our own free decisions, Ellacuría argues that it is necessary to acknowledge and "confront ourselves with" (*enfrentarse*) the real, historical obstacles that we put in the way: the greed, the

---

15. For a more extensive discussion of this concept, see Michael Lee, *Bearing the Weight of Salvation: The Soteriology of Ignacio Ellacuría* (New York: Crossroad, 2009), especially 122-24.

16. See Xavier Zubiri, *Inteligencia sentiente: Inteligencia y realidad* (Madrid: Alianza Editorial, 1991).

17. Ellacuría, "Lectura latinoamericana," 90.

murder, the institutionally entrenched exploitation and abuse of the poor.[18]

One should also consider the kind of self that Ellacuría suggests is implicated in the disclosure of this truth. We are not dealing here with a self that would have to be a learned philosopher (though Ellacuría certainly was one). Nor does this self need to possess any special status within the church or society. Holiness transcends hierarchical office in every sphere. The testimonial self that is called to follow the pattern of Christ could be any Christian and, indeed, any human being: the recipient of the call is *el hombre*.[19] Nevertheless, in order to bear the most authentic witness to the liberating truth that is in question, this self has to accept an extraordinarily demanding calling. This self has to become thoroughly "indifferent" in mind and body, praising, reverencing, and serving God in every thought and action regardless of the consequences. This self has to follow the radical humility and courage of Christ's life, with the expectation that this will likely mean following him even to his death. And this following has to take place within one's present historical situation, however bleak this may be.[20] In short, there are almost no a priori restrictions on the kind of self that is called to bear witness, but this self will be asked to give itself freely, entirely, and concretely to the liberating truth that it discloses. It will have to become a self that is willing to empty itself for the sake of the integral liberation of all creatures, which the triune God both accomplishes and demands.

Finally, it is important to consider more closely how prayer functions as a constitutive source of this sort of testimony. In the end, for Ellacuría, the truth is composed of those Christologically and pneumatologically mediated interactions of divine and human freedom that, by transforming historical reality in liberating ways, give ever-greater glory to God. As we have already noted, the disclosure of this truth requires some kind of practical opposition against the manifold structures of oppressive violence (i.e., sin) that objectively negate it. But what

---

18. For a discussion of the complex notion of *enfrentarse* in Ellacuría, see Kevin Burke, *The Ground beneath the Cross: The Theology of Ignacio Ellacuría* (Washington, DC: Georgetown University Press, 2000), 115.

19. Ellacuría, "Lectura latinoamericana," 68.

20. Ibid., 99.

follows from this observation is not that prayer should in any way be diminished but rather that it must continue unabated even within the various kinds of critical analysis and practice that are required. Ellacuría insists that distinct, recognizable acts of prayer are necessary in order to implicate oneself most deeply in this truth. He argues that the world needs not only a plan for structural change but also, and perhaps even more fundamentally, what he calls a "personal adhesion to the person of Christ."[21] This is a kind of intimacy that he contends will be possible only if prayer is given its "adequate time" as an integral moment of Christian action.[22] All in all, prayer is foundational to the particular kind of *theologal* self that Ellacuría both envisions and becomes. It "lights up" Ellacuría's intellectual and practical works, filling them with the awareness that God's own freedom, freely given to us, is supreme.[23] It gives him the courage to put his life on the line, and indeed to lose it, in fidelity to the *kenotic* but victorious example of the Son.

The Testimony of James Cone

Cone presents a distinct but in many respects similar understanding of Christian testimony in which he draws, however, not on Ignatius but rather on the wisdom of the slaves. This is not to say that Cone's other sources, such as Karl Barth, Paul Tillich, Jürgen Moltmann, and perhaps most crucially of all Martin Luther King Jr. and Malcolm X, are insignificant to his witness. Rather, the point is that these figures help Cone interpret certain theological and practical insights that were first articulated in the sorrowful and joyful songs of the slaves, as well as in the sermons, narratives, and concrete actions that communicated the truth of these songs. Just as Ellacuría's ultimately martyrial testimony took shape through his personal practice of the *Spiritual Exercises,* which began at a relatively young age, so too Cone's testimony started to be formed when he was a young member of the Macedonia A.M.E. Church in Bearden, Arkansas, where he learned to hear and vocalize the hymns of his brutalized ancestors. He gives this period of his life poignant expression in his self-attesting work *My Soul Looks Back.*[24]

---

21. Ibid., 77.

22. Ibid., 104.

23. For Ellacuría's sense of prayer as illumination, see *Fe y justicia*, 209-10.

24. James Cone, *My Soul Looks Back* (Maryknoll, NY: Orbis Books, 1986), 17-40.

Like Ellacuría's Ignatian spirituality, the tradition of black spirituality that Cone retrieves in his life and in his theology (from *Black Theology and Black Power* onward, but especially in and after *The Spirituals and the Blues*) involves a clear sense of Christological conformity.[25] The enslaved authors of the spirituals identify themselves with the life, death, and resurrection of Christ. This identification can be heard in refrains such as "Rise up, shepherd, an' foller"; "Were you there when they crucified my Lord?"; and "Weep no more, Marta, / Weep no more, Mary, / Jesus rise from de dead."[26] Moreover, Cone argues that this spiritual tradition, though ultimately framed by a deep awareness of the love of God that calls all of creation into loving fellowship, also demands a serious confrontation with the sinful structures of the world. Here the idolatrous attachment to riches, honor, and pride that Ignatius exposes in the Meditation on the Two Standards takes on the very particular form of an idolization of whiteness: the worship of a "white god" and the death-dealing accumulation of wealth and power for an exclusively or hegemonically white society.[27]

Against this abomination, which is crystallized but not exhausted by the slave system, Cone opposes not only the loving *kenosis* of the Son but also the recognition that blackness is a crucial part of God's creation and redemption. He goes so far as to affirm that "God is black." This affirmation honors God's compassionate and liberating involvement with the many intrinsically beautiful yet oppressed members of the black diaspora.[28] It is not a question here of how God "looks" (God is invisible) but rather a question of those with whom God identifies in historical situations of white racial domination. Moreover, to say that "Jesus is black," as Cone does, is similarly not to make a statement about his first-century racial identity (an anachronistic notion) but rather to recognize his contemporary presence in the prayers and lives of the many darkly hued, crucified peoples.[29] He

---

25. James Cone, *Black Theology and Black Power* (Maryknoll, NY: Orbis Books, 2008), 94-103, and James Cone, *The Spirituals and the Blues: An Interpretation* (Maryknoll, NY: Orbis Books, 2008).

26. Cone, *The Spirituals and the Blues*, 45-50.

27. Ibid., 20-23.

28. Ibid., 33.

29. James Cone, *A Black Theology of Liberation* (Maryknoll, NY: Orbis Books, 2005), 63-66; and *God of the Oppressed*, 122-26.

is there, together with his Spirit, in the songs of his wounded brothers and sisters.[30]

In Cone's treatment of black spirituality the primary question is not, as it is for Ellacuría, how to make a decision in the midst of prayer that reorients one's life in a solidaristically *kenotic* direction. Rather, the primary question is how to go on believing, struggling, and rejoicing even in the context of extraordinary unmerited suffering. Cone does encourage white Christians to empty themselves and black Christians to give themselves in imitation of Christ, and his black spiritual sources ground his reasoning here. The testimonial sacrifices of Martin, Malcolm, and many others—including many black women such as Nellie Burroughs and Ida B. Wells—support this motif.[31] Black Christians are by no means exempt from the obligation to follow Christ, if necessary, even unto death. But the bulk of the spirituals that Cone interprets seem to be more concerned with sustaining an almost desperate sense of hope that God's promised liberation will one day be a reality than in arriving at any concrete, self-bestowing commitment (or "Election," in the Ignatian sense). These are songs of a downtrodden community that is seeking to preserve its confidence in the gracious activity of the divine liberator, while giving cathartic articulation to its own unspeakable sorrows. These are resilient hymns of praise that are, nevertheless, only a hair's breadth away from the melancholy tones of the blues.[32] The spirituals come close to the doxological lamentations of ancient Israel that appear in Job, the Psalms, and the prophets, which have significantly influenced the comparable theological projects of Johann Baptist Metz and Gustavo Gutiérrez.[33] These songs lay bare the abyssal hearts of an afflicted community. In short, Cone's is not only a spirituality *for* but also *of* the crucified peoples. It is deeply rooted in, and not only compassionately oriented toward, their prayerful cries.

---

30. Cone, *The Spirituals and the Blues*, 2, 42, 49.

31. Cone, *Black Theology and Black Power*, 150; Cone, *Martin & Malcolm & America*, 243; and Cone, *The Cross and the Lynching Tree*, 120-51.

32. Cone, *The Spirituals and the Blues*, 97-127.

33. Ibid., 54-55; see Johann Baptist Metz, *Memoria passionis: Ein provizierendes Gedächtnis in pluralistischer Gesellschaft* (Freiburg im Breisgau: Verlag Herder, 2006), 4-27, and Gustavo Gutiérrez, *On Job: God-Talk and the Suffering of the Innocent*, trans. Matthew J. O'Connell (Maryknoll, NY: Orbis Books, 1987).

This black spiritual tradition engenders a distinctive kind of testimony. As in Ellacuría's case, so too here, the truth that it discloses is not of an abstract philosophical nature.[34] On the contrary, it is the truth of God's love in dialogical relationship with the historical realities of humanity and creation, both in Scripture and in our own contemporary societies. Moreover, once again, this truth partly finds expression through the negation of that which negates it, that is, through a Christic confrontation with sin and death.[35] In Cone's most recent work, *The Cross and the Lynching Tree*, he describes the negativity of the lynching era using Ellacuría's concept of the "crucified peoples of history."[36] In Cone's account, these are human beings whose darkly colored bodies are, in some cases, literally hanging from the trees. Coming face to face with this gruesome reality and working to undo its contemporary reconfigurations (as exhibited, for example, in a racially unjust criminal justice system) are part of the task of Christian witnessing.[37]

Ellacuría and Cone are likewise in some significant agreement regarding the kind of self that is implicated in the disclosure of God's liberating truth. For Cone, as for Ellacuría, this self needs no philosophical, ecclesiastical, or professional credentials. But it does need to make itself radically available to the movements of God's Spirit in history, regardless of the costs, and this is no "easy" vocation. Though similar in this respect, Ellacuría's and Cone's accounts are not entirely the same. Cone adds an importantly different perspective by introducing a black mode of witnessing. To be clear, the blackness of the testimonial self that Cone has in mind is not an exclusionary category but rather a historically specific place of encounter with the living God that is shareable by nonblack persons, whom he exhorts to "become black" with God.[38] His point here is not to define testimony in terms of a racial essence but rather to invite anyone and everyone to share in the hopes and struggles of this widely scorned but divinely beloved community and thereby to bear witness to the truth of God's inseparably liberating and reconciling act of universal love.[39] How-

---

34. Cone, *The Spirituals and the Blues*, 54.

35. Ibid., 67-75.

36. Cone, *The Cross and the Lynching Tree*, xiv.

37. Ibid., 163.

38. Cone, *A Black Theology of Liberation*, 65.

39. Cone, *God of the Oppressed*, 207-25.

ever, along with this genuinely universal aspect of Cone's theology, one can sense a particular concern to uphold the prayerful lives of black Christians, precisely for their sake, and to testify to the liberating presence of God in their midst. This concern is unimpeachable. It reflects a degree of focused energy that is appropriate, given the enormous hardships that have been endured by the black diaspora.

Finally, like Ellacuría, Cone develops an account of Christian witness in which the disclosed truth and the implicated selves that make up this testimony are shown to be centrally dependent on the relationship between divine and human freedom that prayer both generates and sustains. Cone argues, in Johannine fashion, that the truth that sets us free is God's truth. It is nothing other than Jesus Christ himself. Through his saving presence the slaves "could know that they were *people*, even though they were bought and sold like cattle."[40] From the experiences of closeness with Jesus that prayer allowed, the slaves and their descendants received the courage to keep fighting for their God-given freedom, to keep singing and rejoicing even in the midst of collective agony, and to attest with their words and their lives to God's decisive yet still-hidden victory over the life-negating powers of this world. As Cone puts the point, "It does not matter what oppressors say or do or what they try to make us out to be. We know that we have a freedom not made with human hands."[41] A dialogical relationship with God in Christ and the Spirit is an enduring aspect of the testimonial spirituality of black Christians, which connects them permanently to the ultimate source of their freedom. Whatever practical means must be employed to effect real change in the racist structures of society (and these means are certainly necessary), Cone suggests that prayer remains indispensable. There will always be a need to "go down, down in the valley to pray."[42]

Conclusion

There is much more one could say about these two spiritual traditions, Ignatian and black, and about Ellacuría's and Cone's respective ways of employing them to address various contemporary crises. But

---

40. Ibid., 31.
41. Ibid., 129.
42. Cone, *The Spirituals and the Blues*, 59.

what I would like to do now, in conclusion, is reflect briefly on their combined significance. Certainly, when taken together, these two prayerful testimonies have the potential to inspire an integrated form of resistance against socio-economic and racial oppression. The liberating truth of the gospel is a truth that negates both of these negations. Moreover, there is a clear ecumenical potential here. I do not say this only with reference to Catholics and Protestants (although this point is highly significant) but also with reference to Christians who understand themselves as either white or black, Christians who reside in either the North or the South, and Christians of the past and the present. The proximity between Ellacuría and Cone indicates a possible unity of Christian witness that may bridge many of these divides. This is not a unity that erases diversity but rather a unity that can only survive in that extremely fragile place where differences are respected and historical wrongs are righted. This is a place in which the prayers of Ignatius, of the slaves, and of many other holy witnesses can be remembered and affirmed as effective signs of Christ's life in our midst. It is here, I believe, that any compelling sort of Christian testimony can be realized today.

Furthermore, the pairing of Ellacuría and Cone reveals that a full understanding of Christian testimony requires two complementary vocations: a call to *kenosis*, addressed particularly to those who may need to divest themselves of disordered attachments in order to demonstrate a genuine commitment to the liberation of their oppressed brothers and sisters, and a call to steadfast hope, addressed primarily to those already living and struggling to survive on the undersides of history. Prayer, an opening of human freedom to the indomitable freedom of God, is the origin of both of these vocations. The real world of sin, suffering, and death—the concretely violent milieu that demands both critical analysis and practical engagement—is the dangerous arena in which these prayerfully original vocations must be concretely enacted. A theory of witnessing that knows these things surpasses in gravity, it seems to me, any alternative that would be content with a less prayerful, less historical, or less liberating model.

5

Power–Beauty and Prophetic Resistance: A Postcolonial Approach

Agnes M. Brazal

In the 1980s both the Philippines and El Salvador were under author-itarian regimes that were supported by the United States imperial government. In both countries, thousands of people who resisted the repressive rule were tortured and murdered. I was a farmers' com-munity organizer in the early 1980s, and I remember how we would listen to news about El Salvador—the assassination of Archbishop Oscar Romero and, later in 1989, the massacre of the six Jesuit priests, their housekeeper, and her daughter. We felt a deep sense of solidar-ity with those struggling against dictatorial regimes in different parts of the globe, but especially with Latin America, partly because of our common history. As a community organizer, I have also experienced —together with two other female colleagues—being surrounded by five heavily armed men and arrested on the suspicion that we were communists. It was a period of living dangerously, a time that calls for prophets to literally risk their lives.

In this article, I will explore women's prophetic resistance to impe-rial and other forms of domination (as ethnocentrism, sexism, and classism) but viewed through the vernacular lens of the power–beauty dialectic in Philippine culture. I refer to the methodology I am apply-ing as vernacular-postcolonial. Vernacular-postcolonial interpreta-tion makes use of local resources or categories to understand and to "decolonize" our reading of the Bible and the Christian tradition.[1] I

---

1. R. S. Sugirtharajah points out correctly that what can be considered "vernacular" is relative and moveable depending on who is using the term and against whom (*The Bible and the Third World: Precolonial, Colonial and*

shall first engage in a discourse analysis of Philippine representations of the "power–beauty dialectic" in general and in Filipino women's prophetic resistance in particular, and then employ a preferred meaning to re-read prophetic resistance in the book of Judith.[2] I have chosen to focus on Judith because she is a female prophet who deploys her physical and moral beauty as well as strength to resist domination.

Power–Beauty Dialectic

A popular Philippine creation myth narrates the simultaneous emergence of man and woman from a split bamboo stalk, a deep, symbolic expression of the relatively egalitarian relations of women and men in the Philippine islands in precolonial times.[3] However, it was the Spaniards who colonized the Philippines in the sixteenth century who named the first man *Malakas* (meaning "strong," "powerful") and the first woman *Maganda* ("beautiful").[4] While the Spanish identification of the man as powerful and the woman as beautiful may had been intended to impose a complementary and dualistic gender ideology, we find traces of how this power–beauty discourse has been inge-

---

Postcolonial Encounters [Cambridge: Cambridge University Press, 2001], 178-81).

2. Our process of discourse analysis looks at the various representations of a cultural text, the identities linked with these representations, the conditions of their production, their consumption, and to what extent they regulate conduct. See Agnes M. Brazal, "Redeeming the Vernacular: Doing Postcolonial-Intercultural Theological Ethics," *Asian Horizons* 4.1 (June 2010): 50-66. This approach is more akin to the third stream of postcoloniality as identified by R. S. Sugirtharajah. See Sugirtharajah, *The Bible and the Third World*, 248-50.

3. Some precolonial women's rights that Spanish civil law eradicated were "the right to divorce, to have children regardless of marital status, property rights, freedom to contract business arrangements independently of the husband, retention of maiden name, and a central role in religious practices." See Teresita Infante, *The Woman in Early Philippines and among the Cultural Minorities* (Manila: UST Press, 1975). Relative to other countries today, the Philippines ranks no. 5 in the 2013 "Global Gender Gap" report by the World Economic Forum, the only developing country in the top five (http://www.weforum.org/issues/global-gender-gap).

4. In the Visayan region's version of the myth, the man and woman are simply referred to as Sicalac and Sicauay, respectively. See Damiana Eugenio, ed. and compiler, *Philippine Folk Literature: The Myths* (Quezon City: University of the Philippines Press, 1993), 293-96.

niously subverted to represent a more fluid gender relation between women and men.

In a number of contemporary and traditional Philippine discourses, strength is not just identified with men and beauty with women. In the *Diccionario Ingles-Español-Tagalog* by Sofronio Calderon, which was published in 1915, "handsome" is translated in terms that are equivalent to beautiful: *maganda*, *mainam*, and *marikit*. Indeed up to my generation, we describe a handsome man as *magandang lalaki* (literally translated as "attractive man"). Many times, power–beauty operates in Philippine discourses as a duality, more than a dualism where the realities are conceived in oppositional and hierarchical terms. The powerful person is one who exhibits both strength and beauty.[5]

According to the historian Mina Roces, the Philippine female image of power has always been linked to beauty, whether physical or moral.[6] In her analysis of gender and power in post–World War II Philippines, Roces shows how regardless of physical features and so long as she conforms to the expected decorum, a woman associated with political power—either via kinship or by virtue of being elected to a political office—is regarded as beautiful.[7] In turn, physical beauty can also translate into female power, as can be seen from the number of Filipina beauty queen title holders who have become powerful via their marriages to prominent men, or via election or appointment to political positions.

Roces further identifies the emergence of two new symbols of female power during the period of the Marcos dictatorship (1972-1986)—the militant nun and the political activist.[8] These women

5. See Mina Roces, *Women, Power and Kinship Politics: Female Power in Post-War Philippines* (Pasay City: Anvil Publishing, 2000). By power, we here mean the capacity to influence others to act toward a certain direction.

6. Mina Roces, a historian who studied kinship politics in the Philippines, calls for the contextualization of feminism within this cultural narrative instead of simply appropriating radical feminist arguments that valuing women's beauty objectifies them and represents subjugation to men.

7. Roces, *Women, Power and Kinship Politics*, 17. This is possible in the bilateral kinship politics in the Philippines where "power is perceived to be held by the kinship alliance group and not just the persons in office." Ibid., 2.

8. Ibid., 18. Roces distinguishes the militant nun and unarmed activist from the female rebels who took up arms. The latter continued to be subordinated to the Communist Party of the Philippines, which was led mainly by the men.

did not draw their power by being related to a powerful man. They exerted moral power–beauty in their prophetic resistance as they spoke on behalf of and with the victims of martial rule.[9]

The link between beauty and moral goodness is reflected in many Philippine languages. The ethically good is referred to as "beautiful," while moral evil is called "ugly."[10] *Kagandahang-loob* (literally translated as "beautiful inner self" or roughly equivalent to "gracious goodness" or "shared nobility") is, according to the Filipino theological ethicist Dionisio Miranda, the "form" or queen of virtues in the Philippine context.[11] For Filipino psychologist Virgilio Enriquez, *kagandahang-loob* designates an "act of generosity displayed spontaneously on account of the goodness of the heart."[12] Gracious goodness is done out of free will, expecting neither a payment nor a reward, and arising from a genuine concern for the good of the other or the common good.[13]

In oppressive situations, gracious goodness alone is not enough. It has to be accompanied both by *lakas ng loob*, literally "strong inner self" or "courage," and by the strength of collective unity. Enriquez refers to *lakas ng loob* as an "inner resource for change" that enables Filipinos to overcome hardships and engage in cooperative resistance against unjust situations.[14]

---

9. Ibid., 182. While most female politicians do not want to be identified as feminists, this has not been the case among some nuns and political activists who have embraced feminism and integrated feminist theories in their analysis of political and social oppression in the Philippines. Ibid., 107, 133.

10. Leonardo Mercado, *The Filipino Mind: Philippine Philosophical Studies II* (Washington, DC: Council for Research in Values and Philosophy, 1994), 88-89.

11. Dionisio Miranda, SVD, *Buting Pinoy: Probe Essays on Value as Filipino* (Manila: Divine Word Publications, 1992), 177-78.

12. Isabel S. Panopio, *Society and Culture: Introduction to Sociology and Anthropology*, 3rd rev. ed. (Realidad Santico Rolda, Philippines: Katha Publishing, 2007), 90.

13. Leonardo de Castro, "Kagandahang-Loob: Love in Philippine Bioethics," *Eubios Journal of Asian and International Bioethics* 9 (1999): 39-40, http://www.eubios.info/EJ92/ej92e.htm.

14. According to a nationwide psychometric study (1973), *lakas ng loob*, or courage, is among the top seven values of Filipinos. See Virgilio Enriquez, *From Colonial to Liberation Psychology: The Philippine Experience* (Manila: De la Salle University, 1994).

The 1986 People Power revolution that toppled the Marcos dictatorship highlighted the power of beauty combined with strength. Hearts of military men and passive citizens were touched by nonviolent action combined with "attractive" goodness—women giving roses and sandwiches to military men, or citizens volunteering their cars or themselves to block the tanks that were arriving. The strength of unity by a critical mass of Filipinos demonstrated in the People Power revolution and the events leading to it was necessary to exert powerful pressure on the military and the passive citizens to switch alliances, as well as for the United States government to withdraw its support of Ferdinand Marcos.

Power–Beauty in Folk Catholicism

Power–beauty articulations can also be found in Philippine folk Catholic beliefs and practices, particularly in the *Santacruzan* religious procession and the nineteenth-century Christ-image of the revolutionaries.

The *Santacruzan*, which dates back to the Spanish colonial period, is the most widely celebrated folk religious procession in the Philippines. It commemorates the legend of the finding of the cross of Jesus by Queen Helena and Emperor Constantine.[15] The procession features beautiful women representing strong personages of the Bible and in Christian history who have made special contributions to the growth of the faith.

The biblical characters in the procession include women in the Old Testament such as Judith, who beheaded Holofernes to save the Israelites, and Esther, the Jewish queen of Persia, who protected from persecution the exiled Jews in the Persian Empire. Beyond the Old Testament personages are the women who followed Jesus in his pas-

---

15. The historical origins of the *Santacruzan* are not clear though it is generally accepted that it began during the Spanish regime. The story of the cross is popular as well in Mexico, where we hear of the well-known *Auto de cuando Santa Elena halló la Cruz de Nuestro Señor* in 1539. See Nicanor G. Tiongson, "Byzantine Happenings," in *Filipino Heritage: The Making of a Nation*, vol. 7 of *The Spanish Colonial Period (Late 19th Century), The Awakening* (Manila: Lahing Pilipino Publishing, 1978), 1864. See also Teodora T. Battad et al., *Various Religious Beliefs and Practices in the Philippines*, vol. 1 (Manila: Rex Book Store, 2008), 18.

sion and death, such as Mary Magdalene. The highlight of the procession is Queen Helena, with the young Constantine at her side.

The symbols are a mixture of colonial (e.g., Queen Helena and Emperor Constantine) as well as anticolonial figures (e.g., the presence of an anonymous queen of justice, queen of the convicted innocent, and queen lawyer-defender of the poor). In 2009, Amihan, the National Federation of Peasant Women, staged a *Santacruzan* near the gate of the House of Representatives to push for genuine agrarian reform. The queen of the convicted innocent (*Reyna Sentenciada*), tied with a rope and guarded by two soldiers, symbolized the peasants in feudal bondage; the queen lawyer (*Reyna Abogada*) represented those who defend the poor and the oppressed; and the queen of justice (*Reyna Justicia*) symbolized the elusive justice for landless farmers. *Reyna Fe* (faith), *Reyna Sporrans*, and ten children dressed in white garb represented faith, hope, and collective unity and the struggle to attain genuine agrarian reform. Queen Helena's finding of the cross symbolized victory, and instead of the usual flowers, the women carried agricultural products such as vegetables, root crops, and so on. The gate of the House of Representatives had been transformed into "a fashion runway" as Amihan members in evening gown attire paraded carrying "messages like genuine land reform, pass HB 3059, stop corruption, end poverty and hunger, stop extrajudicial killings."[16]

While the celebration of the *Santacruzan* on other occasions has degenerated into a mere fashion show or a tourist spectacle,[17] this should not prevent us from appreciating and reappropriating the liberating insights of the people's religious practice—that is, the celebration of female power in the history of salvation, the conviction that women of faith and courage are "beautiful," and Filipino women's prophetic use of power–beauty to denounce oppression!

---

16. D'Jay Lazaro, "Women Group Holds Santacruzan at Batasan to Push for Genuine Agrarian Reform," *GMA News,* May 13, 2009, http://www.gmanetwork.com/news/story/161159/news/nation/women-group-holds-santacruzan-at-batasan-to-push-for-agrarian-reform.

17. Rachel A. R. Bundang, "'This Is Not Your Mother's Catholic Church': When Filipino Catholic Spirituality Meets American Culture," in *Pinay Power: Peminist Critical Theory,* ed. Melinda L. de Jesús (New York: Routledge, 2005), 69.

This power–beauty dialectic is also exemplified in the image of Christ of the nineteenth-century revolutionaries against imperial Spain,[18] who associated the powers of Christ with his "beautiful *loob*," which is not only pure and controlled but attracts others in its graciousness. As powerful talismans are believed to emit light and make their possessors radiant,[19] Christ himself has been described in the *Pasyon* as radiating light.[20] Only a person with a "beautiful inner self that attracts others" can be a light to others. A "beautiful *loob*" includes following the straight path and exhibiting compassion.[21]

In the Philippine indigenous perspective, however, power is believed to permeate everything and can be concentrated in certain objects (talismans) or individuals referred to as "men of prowess."[22] In a transfer of power, the gain of one in power means the loss of another. This traditional concept of power tends to reinforce hierarchical structures. The notion that the amount of power in the universe is limited and that only a few (e.g., the wealthy, the priests) can accumulate power can justify patron–client relationships both in the church and in society at large.[23]

Classical Western juridical theory has held a similar view; it regards power as a right (a commodity) that one possesses and that

---

18. It was in the singing of the *Pasyon* during Holy Week that the revolutionaries fighting the Spanish colonizers made this link. The *Pasyon* is a narration of the history of salvation from creation to the second coming of Christ, with particular focus on the passion, death, and resurrection. See Reynaldo Ileto, *Pasyon and Revolution: Popular Movements in the Philippines, 1840-1910* (Quezon City: Ateneo de Manila University Press, 1979).

19. Ibid., 41.

20. Ibid., 45.

21. Ibid., 86, 180.

22. The Philippines shares this belief with other Southeast Asian countries such as Indonesia. See Benedict R. O'G Anderson, "The Idea of Power in Javanese Culture," in *Culture and Politics in Indonesia*, ed. Claire Holt, Benedict R. O'G Anderson, and James Siegel (Ithaca, NY: Cornell University Press, 1972), 1-70. See also Herminia Meñez's chapter "Talismanic Magic and Political Leadership," in her book *Explorations in Philippines Folklore* (Quezon City: Ateneo de Manila University Press, 1996), 97-98.

23. That power can be concentrated in certain things (e.g., saints, hosts) that its possessor may absorb also reinforces superstitious beliefs and overreliance on amulets and talismans.

can be transferred to another via a legal act or contract.[24] Contemporary theorists, though, have moved away from this view of power as a "substance" that can be fixed in an individual. As Michel Foucault notes, power is a "relation of force."[25] Power is continuously flowing, depending on the negotiations, relations, and competition between groups, institutions, and discourse, even if some individuals may have greater capacities to influence the forces of power.

Sacred power, like social power, is also a "relation of force" that is present whenever power is utilized to attain mutuality or right relations—to generate greater "power with" so that we can live more just and compassionate lives.[26] Rita Nakashima Brock speaks of this sacred power as erotic power[27] so as to stress the attraction to beauty that it involves, as well as its goal of mutuality. In Jesus' life, we see erotic, that is, attractive, power at work as he himself was nurtured and formed by his family and friends. What we see in Jesus' ministry is not a unilateral transfer of power from the powerful to the powerless but of power in mutual relation at work. His interaction with women, non-Jews, and sinners helped form his vision of the *basilēia* of God. One of the first things he did was to call others to join him in a union of men and women to help generate "more power with" to realize the *basilēia* of God. It is in fact erotic power that we also witnessed at play during the 1986 People Power revolution, as goodness attracted others to act in solidarity in dismantling the dictatorship.

Power–Beauty and Prophetic Resistance in Judith

One of the beautiful and powerful biblical women represented in the *Santacruzan,* and rightfully referred to as a prophet, is Judith. In this section, we shall use the Philippine power–beauty dialectic as a lens to re-read the story of Judith.

The prophet is God's spokesperson, one who reminds kings and other leaders and the ordinary Israelites of their covenant with God.

---

24. Michel Foucault, *Power/Knowledge: Selected Interviews and Other Writings 1972-1977,* ed. Colin Gordon (New York: Pantheon Books, 1980), 88.

25. Ibid., 98.

26. Carter Heyward, *Saving Jesus from Those Who Are Right: Rethinking What It Means to Be Christian* (Minneapolis: Fortress Press, 1999), 55.

27. Rita Nakashima Brock, *Journeys by Heart: A Christology of Erotic Power* (New York: Crossroad, 1991).

Prophecy is also a fruit of the spiritual and ethical maturation of a person whereby wisdom, or Sophia, rests upon the prophet. Prophecy and wisdom are, in the later books of the Hebrew Bible, deeply intertwined. For example, Sophia herself in the book of Proverbs is described in a manner similar to the prophets of ancient Israel, standing in a public place, chastising the people and warning them of the consequences of ignoring her words (Proverbs 1:2-33).[28]

In the *Wisdom of Solomon*, which was written near the time of Jesus, Sophia is not just sent by God but is the very personification of God's self.[29] God personified as Sophia manifests, as one says in Tagalog, a *lakas* (power) guided by *ganda* (gracious goodness). Spirit-Sophia is "a breath of the power of God," (*Wisdom* 7:23, 25), the "active cause of all things" (8:5). At the same time, she is "holy" and "humane" (7:22-23), an image of God's gracious goodness (7:29; Proverbs 8:20). She is both powerful and merciful (*Wisdom* 11:21-26). She led the Israelites in resisting oppression out of Egypt and through the desert, because of her boundless compassion (*Wisdom* 10-11). *Wisdom of Solomon* 7:27 further states that "In every generation she passes into holy souls and makes them friends of God and prophets."

The biblical character of Judith has also been related by various authors to wisdom,[30] and we can well argue that she is a prophet of Sophia.[31] Judith is not only physically beautiful (Judith 8:7; 10:7, 14, 21,

---

28. Marcus Borg, *Meeting Jesus Again for the First Time: The Historical Jesus and the Heart of Contemporary Faith* (New York: HarperSan Francisco, 1994), 98-99.

29. Elizabeth Johnson, *She Who Is: Mystery of God in Feminist Theological Discourse* (New York: Crossroad, 1992), 91-92; Elisabeth Schüssler Fiorenza, *In Memory of Her* (New York: Crossroad, 1985), 132. For a list of recent scholarship on this, see Marcus Borg's chapter "Jesus the Wisdom of God: Sophia Become Flesh," in his *Meeting Jesus Again*, 113 n. 23.

30. Judith's ways have been compared to female Wisdom in Proverbs 8 (see esp. Proverbs 8:10). See, e.g., Linda Day's introduction to the book of Judith in the *New Oxford Annotated Bible: New Revised Standard Version with the Apocrypha*, ed. Michael D. Coogan et al.; aug. 3rd ed. (Oxford: Oxford University Press, 2007), 32-33 (Apocrypha Section).

31. Robin Gallher Branchi refers to Judith as a "prophetess" more for her visions of the future that come true (Judith 8:32; 10:9; 12:18; 14:3-4). See her article "Judith: A Remarkable Heroine, Part 2," *Bible History Daily*, August 1, 2012, http://www.biblicalarchaeology.org/daily/people-cultures-in-the-bible/people-in-the-bible/judith-a-remarkable-heroine-part-2/.

23) but also morally so (she feared God with great devotion, according to 8:8).[32] That "no one spoke ill of her" despite her beauty and wealth (8:7) suggests a graciousness that can dispel envy or jealousy even from other women.[33] People recognize her "beautiful *loob*" and her wisdom, which has been nurtured from the beginning of her life.

The narrative or fictional story of Judith begins with the "Assyrian" imperial campaign to expand its territories and take revenge against nations that resist surrender (Judith 1-3).[34] Cut off from their water supply, the Israelites in Bethulia who initially opposed the occupation planned to finally surrender (7:16-28). When Judith learns of this, she calls the town's elders and boldly tells them that it is a mistake to surrender (8:9-27). She speaks to them[35] in the manner of Sophia and the prophets, that is, with authority and courage[36] using the introductory words, "Listen to me" (8:11). [37] Like Sophia, she tells them what is right (Proverbs 8:6). She devises a plan that she and her maid execute. They cross the enemy's territory courageously, mislead them, and decapitate Holofernes, the head of the Assyrian conquering army (10:1-13:8). Like

---

32. The Greek word for "beautiful" is *kalos*. It can refer not only to physical beauty but to inner goodness as well; that which is "attractively good," as in *kagandahang-loob*, or a "good that inspires (motivates) others to embrace what is lovely (beautiful, praiseworthy)" (Bible Hub by Biblos, http://biblesuite.com/greek/2570.htm).

33. Branchi, "Judith."

34. The narrative about Judith is fiction (a Jewish novel in the Graeco-Roman period) and to be characterized as a wisdom story. See Denise Dombkowski Hopkins, "Judith," in *Women's Bible Commentary: Expanded Edition with Apocrypha*, ed. Carol A. Newsom and Sharon H. Ringe (Louisville: Westminster John Knox Press, 1998), 279-85. The book is set in the imperial rule of Nebuchadnezzar, who ruled the "Assyrians" (Judith 1:1, 13; 2:1), though this is contradicted by allusions to the exilic return (4:3; 5:19). The book of Judith was probably written during the Hasmonean dynasty in the second century BCE or early first century BCE (165-137 BCE).

35. *Women's Bible Commentary: Expanded Edition with Apocrypha*, ed. Carol A. Newsom and Sharon H. Ringe (Louisville: Westminster John Knox Press, 1998), 283; see also Hopkins, "Judith," 282-83.

36. See Proverbs 1:8, 20-21, 23; 5:1; 8:6, 32, 36.

37. E.g., Judith 8:11, "Listen to me, rulers of the people of Bethulia!"; 8:32, "Listen to me. I am about to do something that will go down through all generations of our descendants"; and 14:1, "Listen to me, my brethren, and take this head and hang it upon the parapet of your wall."

Sophia who liberated the Israelites from Egyptian slavery (*Wisdom* 10-11), Judith helps deliver the Israelites from Assyrian oppression.

According to Philippine power–beauty categories, Judith acts out of gracious goodness (*kagandahang loob*). On her own initiative she risks her life,[38] so that Israel may remain faithful to its covenant with *Adonai* (YHWH), its only king. She draws courage (*lakas ng loob*) in her prayer, "O God, my God, hear me also, a widow" (Judith 9:4), appealing to the God of the poor and the marginalized before executing her plan (9:11), and again asking God for strength prior to beheading Holofernes (13:8-9). The combination of courage and beauty she manifests generate greater "power with" and rally the Israelites to act in solidarity to finally thwart their enemies (15:4-5). And thus, in the victory dance honoring her,[39] Judith does not simply sit and watch as the main honoree, nor does she simply accept the high priest Joachim's remark, "You have done all this with your own hand" (15:10). Instead, she joins and leads the women in the dancing, signifying as well that she recognizes that she did not save Israel as a "lone ranger" but that this is a victory ultimately brought about by communal solidarity of men and women alike. In her song of praise, she not only gives due to God "who crushes wars" (15:2) but acknowledges as well the participation of the "sons of slave girls" (15:11-12).

Judith models prophetic resistance to imperial forces, which symbolize the weak. Through a combination of gracious goodness and courage, she inspires unity and solidarity and defeats the mighty. There is an ambivalence, though, to what extent she is an exemplar today against other forms of domination, such as patriarchy[40] and ethnocentrism. On the one hand, she has indeed shown herself to be a strong woman who speaks with wisdom and authority and is not afraid to criticize the male elders or leaders.[41] She herself conceives

---

38. See Judith 13:20: "because you did not spare your own life when our nation was brought low."

39. See "Dance," Jewish Virtual Library, http://www.jewishvirtuallibrary. org/jsource/judaica/ejud_0002_0005_0_04849.html, under the section "Ancient Israel."

40. See also Amy-Jill Levine, "Sacrifice and Salvation: Otherness and Domestication in the Book of Judith," in *"No One spoke Ill of Her": Essays on Judith*, ed. James C. VanderKam (Atlanta: Scholars Press, 1992), 17-30.

41. That this was threatening to first-century patriarchal society is suggested

a plan, capitalizing on her beauty,[42] and after its successful accomplishment, commands the Israelites with respect to how to overcome their enemies. Her "goodness" is erotic; that is, it inspires solidarity and prophetic resistance. She also recognizes that her female slave deserves freedom, and she releases her (16:23).[43]

On the other hand, Judith returns back to the "private" space of the home after the victory is won. There is an absence of any indication in the text of her questioning the all-male leadership structure in her time.[44] She sees the captivity of the Shechemite women and their daugh-

---

in Clement's letter to the Corinthians (*1 Clement* 55:3-5), when contrary to what the text of Judith says, he writes: "Many women, empowered by God's grace, have performed deeds worthy of men. The blessed Judith, when her city was under siege, begged of the elders to be permitted to leave it for the enemy's camp" (*Early Christian Fathers,* ed. Cyril C. Richardson [New York: Touchstone, 1996], 68). The biblical text narrates that Judith did not even inform the leaders of her plan and simply told them that she would leave to do her mission (Judith 8:32-34; 10:9-10). See Jan Willem Van Henten, "Judith as Alternative Leader: A Rereading of Judith 7-13," in *A Feminist Companion to Esther, Judith and Susanna,* ed. Athalya Brenner (New York: T. & T Clark, 1995), 224-52, at 246-47.

42. Many Western feminists view beauty practices as contributing to the production and regulation of femininity and maintaining the unequal power relations between the sexes and among women. Beauty in fact has not generally been considered a worthy subject for feminist investigation, and instead, feminists opt to speak about the body. Some changes though have been noted by Rita Felski, who has reviewed some contemporary writings on beauty. She claims that "the trajectory of feminist work on beauty has shown a distinct (though far from unanimous) shift from the rhetoric of victimization and oppression to an alternative language of empowerment and resistance." See Rita Felski, "'Because It Is Beautiful': New Feminist Perspectives on Beauty," *Feminist Theory* 7.2 (2006): 273-82, at 280. Among the few female theologians who have written on beauty from a feminist perspective are Susan Ross, *For the Beauty of the Earth: Women, Sacramentality, and Justice* (New York: Paulist Press, 2006); Susan Ross, "Women, Beauty and Justice: Moving Beyond von Balthasar," *Journal of the Society of Christian Ethics* 25.1 (2005): 79-98; and Michelle A. González, *Sor Juana: Beauty and Justice in the Americas* (Maryknoll, NY: Orbis Books, 2003).

43. Though we do not hear the voice of the nameless maid in the text, Judith's concern for her might indicate that Judith inquired of her willingness to assist her in her mission and that she voluntarily consented. See Branchi, "Judith."

44. Musa Dube, "Rahab Says Hello to Judith: A Decolonizing Feminist Reading," in *Toward a New Heaven and a New Earth: Elizabeth Schüssler Fiorenza,* ed. Fernando F. Segovia, (Maryknoll, NY: Orbis Books, 2003), 54-72.

ters as booty and the killing of their slaves as part of God's plan.[45] She does not raise a voice of protest when the rest of the people of Bethulia plunder the Assyrian camp and seize a large amount of booty (15:6-7, 11). Though unlike them, she did not keep the booty from Holofernes's property to enrich herself but offered them back to God. (16:19).

Conclusion

Our postcolonial discourse analysis has shown links between beauty and the Philippine image of power. Proximity to power makes a woman beautiful, while beauty, whether moral or physical, is a source of power. In the *Santacruzan* procession, Filipinos celebrate biblical women of power and of beauty. A group of peasant women has even reinvented this tradition as a form of protest against feudal bondage. Philippine revolutionary folk Catholicism has also highlighted the power of Christ's gracious goodness and the fact that sacred power is guided by moral beauty. For women's use of power to be truly liberating, however, there is a need to shift from the understanding of power as accumulated by and concentrated in the hands of a few individuals to the notion of power as erotic, attracting others toward solidarity and mutuality, as manifested in Jesus' relations and ministry and demonstrated as well in the 1986 People Power revolution.

The story of Judith, one of the main characters in the *Santacruzan*, can be re-read from this understanding of the power–beauty dialectic. While the Assyrians who bully the other nations deploy a power devoid of beauty, Judith's prophetic resistance embodies the power–beauty of wisdom-Sophia, which unites the Israelites in solidarity and cooperative resistance against Assyrian domination. Judith—though falling short of fully challenging patriarchal and ethnocentric structures—can represent those who are able to overcome domination because of their faith in God's strength and beauty within them.

---

45. In a prayer recalling God avenging the rape of Dinah, she says, "You gave up their wives for booty and their daughters to captivity, and all their booty to be divided among your beloved children who burned with zeal for you and abhorred the pollution of their blood and called on you for help. O God, my God, hear me also, a widow" (Judith 9:4).

6

The Witness of the Church at the Side of the Poor: The Past and Present of a Theology of Liberation

Paulo Fernando Carneiro de Andrade

The Beginnings of the Theology of Liberation

Latin American theology of liberation arises as a theological expression of the church's commitment to the poor. In order to understand the genesis of this theology produced in Latin America, one has to remember the genuine Copernican revolution of the church in the twentieth century promoted by the Second Vatican Council. From the outset, the council focused in a seminal way on the church as truly global, plural, and non-European.

In the decades preceding the Second Vatican Council, contextualized theologies began to be formulated in a new way and with unprecedented vigor.[1] The council valorized cultural diversity and

---

1. In Catholic circles, the explicit demand for an academic contextual theology was first raised around the year 1955 by a group of priests from Haiti and Africa. In spite of this, the hegemony of the then-prevailing manualistic theology lasted at least until the Second Vatican Council. Such theology, formulated from the paradigms of traditional European culture, survived to the 1960s, primarily because the prevalence in the Catholic environment of antimodernist sentiments, which inhibited or even arrested the introduction of some fundamental questions of modernity into Catholic thought, the efforts of some theological sectors notwithstanding. See Marcel Chappin, "Contextual Theology," in *Dictionary of Fundamental Theology,* ed. René Latourelle and Rino Fisichella (New York: Crossroad, 1995), 1097-98. For an overview of twentieth-century theology, see Rosino Gibellini, *La teologia del XX secolo* (Brescia: Queriniana, 1992).

affirmed the local church, a direct fruit of the ecclesiological paradigms "Church as People of God" and "Church as Communion."[2]

On the one hand, a theology of liberation was made possible by the de-centering produced by the council, and, on the other hand, we cannot understand its development without remembering the movement arising from the bosom of the Second Vatican Council that came to be known as "The Church of the Poor." The question of poverty motivated a group of council fathers to adopt a commitment to the poor and a simple way of life. This commitment was expressed in a document known as "Pacta das catacumbas da igreja serva e pobre" ("The Catacomb Pact of the Poor Servant Church"), signed by about forty council fathers on November 16, 1965, after the Eucharistic celebration in the catacombs of St. Domatila; it revealed an important dimension of the spirit of the council.[3] Although the signatories chose not to divulge their names, it is known that Dom Hélder Câmera played a leading role among them. This same spirit led a large number of priests and religious in the 1960s to embrace a new lifestyle and to establish communities that inserted themselves into the midst of the working class, that is, sharing housing conditions with the poor and bearing witness to the everyday suffering of the marginalized and the exploited. These persons, as a result of the experience of sharing their lives with the poor, no longer accepted traditional explanations of the causes of poverty and moved on to understand it as the product of exploitation and oppression. At that point the question arose: "How are we going to be Christians in a continent of the exploited and oppressed poor?" Thus, a space was created for participation in the movements of liberation and popular organization.

The theme of liberation already present in certain pastoral settings was accepted by the episcopal conference of Latin America that met in 1968 in Medellín in the Second General Conference of Latin American Bishops. This meeting had as its objective the promotion of the Second Vatican Council's application to the Latin American reality.[4]

---

2. On the debate concerning the ecclesiology of the "People of God," see José Comblin, *People of God*, trans. Phillip Berryman (Maryknoll, NY: Orbis Books, 2004).

3. See Boaventura Kloppenburg, ed., *Concílio Vaticano II. Vol. V, Quarta Sessão* (Petrópolis: Vozes, 1966), 526-28.

4. Several pastoral documents since 1966 have used the term "liberation"

At the same time, the first essays were published in which the phrase *theology of liberation* can be found.[5] The first conference on a theology of liberation took place in 1970 in Bogota. It was at this time understood as a theology that had as its objective a specific reality or theme, namely, at once political, social, and economic liberation ("a theology of genitives," so to speak).[6] It fell to Gustavo Gutiérrez in 1971 to lay the groundwork for this theology as a systematic theology, that is, one that treated liberation as an optic or lens and not as a mere object of research. This took place with the publication of his work *Teología de la liberación: Perspectivas*.[7] At almost the same time, Leonardo Boff published his Christology *Jesus Cristo Libertador,* and Hugo Assman released an anthology that had the same perspective as Gutiérrez.[8] These were the beginnings of a theology of liberation.

The 1970s and the Development of the Method of a Theology of Liberation

The growth or development of the theology of liberation through the course of the 1970s can be divided into two phases. The first, between the years 1971 and 1974, corresponds to the years of its articulation,

---

in a sociological sense, arising from theories of dependency. Some of these are collected in Juan José Rossi, *Iglesia latinoamericana: Protesta o profecia?* (Avellaneda, Argentina: Busqueda, 1969).

5. On this point, see Rubem A. Alves, "Towards a Theology of Liberation" (Ph.D. diss., Princeton University, 1968), and Richard Shaull, "La liberation humana desde uma perspectiva teológica," *Mensaje* 168 (1968): 175-79; see also Hugo Assmann, "Tarefas e limitações de uma teologia do desenvolvimento," *Vozes* 62 (1968): 13-21, in which the author practically established the program for the future of liberation theology.

6. See Paulo Fernando Carneiro de Andrade, *Fé e eficácia* (São Paulo: Loyola, 1991), 57.

7. Gustavo Gutiérrez, *Theology of Liberation: History, Politics, and Salvation,* trans. Sister Caridad Inda, John Eagleson, and Matthew J. O'Connell; rev. ed. (Maryknoll, NY: Orbis Books, 2009), originally published as *Teología de la liberación: Perspectivas* (Lima: Centro de Estudios y Publicaciones, 1971).

8. Hugo Assmann, ed., *Opresión-liberación: Desafio de los cristianos* (Montevideo: Tierra Nueva, 1971); Leonardo Boff, *Jesus Christ Liberator: A Critical Christology for Our Time* (Maryknoll, NY: Orbis Books, 1978), originally published as a series of articles in *Grande Sinal* 25 (1971), and subsequently as *Jesus Cristo Libertador* (Petrópolis: Vozes, 1972).

and the second, which takes place between 1975 and 1979, could be called the period of maturation in the midst of growing criticism from certain ecclesial sectors. From the outset, a theology of liberation understood itself to be a new way of doing theology that took as its point of departure the theological unfolding of a concrete historical social reality, namely, the situation of poverty that one finds in Latin America. One novel element in this method is the explicit (and therefore critical) use of sociological, rather than philosophical, mediation in order to interpret this reality. A majority of the theologians opted for a sociology that privileged a structural reading of reality. This reading resulted in conflict-oriented analyses—even on the level of economics—as opposed to other sociological mediations that highlighted organic social realities, some aspect of culture, or individual agency. What resulted was called a "Marxist" analysis, a name that caused not a few problems.

Despite encountering resistance, a theology of liberation proceeded on its own trajectory. In 1974, the journal *Concilium* published a special issue entirely dedicated to this theme. It dealt with the international recognition of this theology, which had already in 1972 been the theme of a colloquium in Spain at Escorial.[9] One can say that this initial moment was a new phase for the progress of this theology that henceforth will focus more precisely on the question of method.

In the course of the two years 1976 and 1977, following the publication of the doctoral thesis of Clodovis Boff, who returned that year from Louvain to Brazil, the main elements of the theological method of the theology of liberation came to be established.[10] Clodovis Boff proposed as a solution for the question of the articulation

---

9. According to Roger Vekemans, the best-known international recognition of liberation theology is obviously issue 96 (June 1974) of *Concilium*, entirely dedicated to it, under the title *Práxis de libertação e fé cristã o testemunho dos teólogos latino-americanos*. See Roger Vekmans, "Expansion mundial de la teología de la liberación latinoamericana," in Consejo episcopal latinoamericano (CELAM), *Socialismo y socialismos em América latina* (Bogotá, 1977), 269-319, 318.

10. Clodovis Boff, "Teologia e prática," in *Revista eclesiástica brasileira* 144 (1976): 789-810; Boff, *Teologia e prática: A teologia do político e suas mediações* (Petrópolis: Vozes, 1977) (Eng. trans, *Theology and Praxis* [Maryknoll, NY: Orbis Books, 1987]).

between sociological and theological modes of knowing (*saber soci-ológico e teológico*) the recognition of a political theology (of which, as he then thought, a theology of liberation constituted a particular species[11]) that was established by the articulation of two mediations: a social-analytical one that produces a material object distinct from the social-economic-political reality in itself, and a hermeneutic mediation that establishes a form object to determine its relevance. These two mediations have to respect each other with regard to the relative autonomy of the two disciplinary fields, and one must avoid both an instrumentalization of the social-analytical mediation and a subordination of the hermeneutic mediation to any other mediation. In this sense, the common characterization of a theology of libera-tion as a "theology born from praxis" does not have to be understood in a sense that would contradict the fundamental truth that all the-ology is a reflection of the faith for the purpose of illuminating the proclaimed and practiced faith (it is simultaneously *understanding seeking faith* and *faith seeking understanding; believing to understand, understanding to believe*). In this sense, a theology of liberation, like any theology, is born from faith. Christian faith is the point of departure that gives it its relevance and constitutes its discourse as theological. As Gustavo Gutiérrez observed in his very first book, a theology of liberation derives from a question posed to the faith about the meaning of Christian existence in a continent of those who have been despoiled and oppressed.[12] Faith is thus the point of depar-ture and the point of arrival; to affirm that this is a "theology born of praxis," therefore, does not establish praxis as its formal object but rather recognizes praxis as its material object. One must here recognize that this method was not constituted to investigate real-ity in itself; rather, it always existed to interpret reality critically. In this sense, one should also note that the socio-analytic mediation is finally indissoluble from the constitution of the material object.

---

11. Boff subsequently changed his mind, regarding liberation theology as a global theological system, in line with G. Gutiérrez, L. Boff, J. B. Libânio, and others. His conclusions, however, remain valid for the core of liberation theology inasmuch as it is political theology. See Clodovis Boff, "Retrato de 15 anos da teologia da libertação," in *Revista eclesiástica brasileira* 182 (1986): 263-71.

12. See the introduction to Gutiérrez, *Teología de la liberación: Perspectivas*, Lima: Centro de Estudios y Publicaciones 1971 (see n. 7 above).

A deficient socio-analytic mediation, not critically controlled and therefore susceptible to becoming markedly ideological, would lead to the constitution of a material object that could result in misleading theological conclusions. Clodovis Boff's dissertation rapidly earned a consensus among most of the theologians who were at that time producing a theology of liberation.

The Puebla conference was convened to celebrate the tenth anniversary of the conference at Medellín and to assess the course of the Latin American Catholic Church over that period, as well as to reflect on new pastoral exigencies. The preparation for Puebla inaugurated at the end of the 1970s a new phase in the debate about a theology of liberation, focused above all on the employment of so-called Marxist analysis and socio-analytic mediation. Although the final document from the meeting at Puebla did not name a theology of liberation as such, it stated,

> one must take note here of the ideologization to which one exposes theological reflection when it takes its point of departure from a praxis that takes recourse to Marxist analysis.[13]

The danger, according to this document, would be a rationalism in which faith was subordinated to reason. Shortly thereafter followed a more exacerbated criticism of the theology of liberation.

The 1980s and the Critical Reception of a Theology of Liberation

In August 1984, the Congregation for the Doctrine of the Faith published a document entitled *Libertatis nuntius*. This document had as its principal objective "to draw the attention of pastors, theologians, and all the faithful to the deviations, and risks of deviation, damaging to the faith and to Christian living, that are brought about by certain forms of the theology of liberation which use, in an insufficiently critical manner, concepts borrowed from various currents of Marxist thought."[14] The document consisted of two parts: a first, positive

---

13. Final Document of CELAM Meeting at Puebla, 1979, #545.

14. "Introduction," in Congregation for the Doctrine of the Faith, "Instruction on Certain Aspects of the 'Theology of Liberation,'" August 6, 1984, accessed

part (chaps. 1-5) and a second part, which noted the problems of one current of the theology of liberation of a Marxist bent without citing any specific authors (chaps. 6-11). In the second part there is a chapter dedicated to Marxist analysis (chap. 7) and two other chapters that treat the implications of its use: violence and subversion of the sense of the truth (chap. 8) and theological rationalism (chap. 9). In 1986 the Congregation for the Doctrine of the Faith published a second document on this question entitled *Libertatis conscientia*. The second document had been anticipated since the promulgation of the first instruction and was intended to present the theme of liberation in a positive tone, emphasizing those elements that were found to be in concordance with the Catholic ecclesial tradition. It should be emphasized that this latter instruction used the same method that was used at Medellín and Puebla and that is the authentic basis of the theology of liberation, namely, the "see, judge, and act" method. In this sense, it did not find any possible perversion of a theology of liberation to be inherent in its original method.

A few months after the promulgation of this document, a letter also appeared from the Holy Father to the Brazilian bishops that was dated April 9, 1986, and concluded the *Visita ad limina* made by the bishops from Brazil in the course of 1985 and in the beginning of 1986. In this letter the pontiff made reference to the two Vatican instructions, not only reaffirming their importance but also recognizing the value of the Brazilian social pastoral activity and the centrality of a love for the poor that was neither exclusive nor excluding.[15] The Holy Father also exhorted pastors that they help "to remain unflaggingly vigilant that this correct and necessary theology of liberation evolves in Brazil and in Latin America in a manner homogenous and not heterogenous with the theology of all epochs and in complete fidelity to the doctrine of the church, remaining attentive to a preferential love that neither excludes nor is exclusive to the poor."[16]

---

on-line at http://www.vatican.va/roman_curia/congregations/cfaith/documents/rc_con_cfaith_doc_19840806_theology-liberation_en.html on March 19, 2014.

15. Letter of the Holy Father to the episcopal conference of the bishops of Brazil, #3, accessed on-line at http://www.va/holy_father/john_paul_ii/letters/1986/documents/hf_jp-ii_let_19860409_conf-episcopale-brasile_po.html on March 19, 2014.

16. Ibid., #5.

The promulgation of the social encyclical *Sollicitudo rei socialis* represented the high point of the reception of the theology of liberation by the Roman magisterium. In its conclusion the pontiff affirms:

> Recently, in the period following the publication of the encyclical *Populorum progressio*, a new way of confronting the problems of poverty and underdevelopment has spread in some areas of the world, especially in Latin America. This approach makes liberation the fundamental category and the first principle of action. The positive values, as well as the deviations and risks of deviation that are damaging to the faith and are connected with this form of theological reflection and method, have been appropriately pointed out by the Church's Magisterium.[17]

The events of 1989 precipitated, among other things, the development of a new phase of the theology of liberation.

A Theology of Liberation and the Crisis of Paradigms

The fall of the Berlin wall in 1989 marked the end of real socialism. The collapse of Soviet socialism was more than simply the fall of an economic system; in conjunction with the process of economic globalization and the crisis of modernity, it precipitated a crisis of paradigms. In Western capitalism, the regime of Fordist accumulation had entered into a crisis beginning in the mid-1970s.[18] The crisis of this regime of accumulation was accompanied by an intense process of deregulation and by the rise of a regime of flexible accumulation that called into question the great social achievements of the postwar era that constituted the social welfare state in both its American and European versions.[19] The relaxation of labor laws and the removal of barriers to the circulation of capital, goods, and services effected by the regime of unrestricted accumulation did not occur independently within each individual state. On the contrary, a large part of the West-

---

17. *Sollicitudo rei socialis* #46.

18. See Alain Lipietz, "New Tendencies in the International Division of Labor: Regimes of Accumulation and Modes of Regulation," in *Production, Work, Territory: The Geographical Anatomy of Industrial Capitalism*, ed. Allen John Scott and Michael Storper (Boston: Allen & Unwin, 1986), 16-40.

19. David Harvey, *The Condition of Postmodernity: An Enquiry into the Origins of Cultural Change* (1980; repr. Cambridge, MA: Blackwell, 1994).

ern global economy generated the phenomenon of neoliberal global-ization more or less all at once.[20]

The transformation of the Fordist–Western economy, accompa-nied by its corollary phenomenon of neoliberal globalization, was linked with a profound crisis of culture hegemonically associated with industrial capitalism: modernity and its enlightenment matrix. With the surpassing of the industrial–Fordist society, the culture that was simultaneously its expression and its promoter also exhausted itself.

On the one hand, the crisis of Fordism in the 1970s finally placed in check in a clear way the ideas of the progress and universal value of modern reason. On the other hand, the very nature of the post-Fordist economy required the rupturing of the predominately linear and homogenizing logic of Enlightenment modernity. This culture had in a certain way already been contested at the end of the 1960s by some avant-garde sectors such as the hippie movement, and it progressively lost plausibility starting in the 1980s.[21] The fall of Soviet socialism ultimately also contributed to this crisis, because the crisis of Enlightenment modernity is a crisis of its own paradigm and the historical projects associated with it.

These great changes in the 1990s ultimately brought about the "end of the world as we know it" and gave rise to a crisis of paradigms in the social sciences and in utopian thought.[22] This crisis affects the theology of liberation not only by impinging directly on its mate-rial object but even more because it is a crisis of the culture from which the theology of liberation was born. One could even say that the theology of liberation, like so many other theologies of the twen-tieth century, was established in dialogue with modernity and is in a certain sense the product of that culture. The loss of the plausibility of modern culture directly affected all discourses produced within this culture, including religious discourses. The process of implementing neoliberal policies brought a profound crisis of political action and

---

20. David Harvey, *Spaces of Global Capitalism: Towards a Theory of Uneven Geographical Development* (New York: Verso, 2006).

21. See Steven Best and Douglas Kellner, *Postmodern Theory: Critical Interrogations* (Houndmills: Macmillan, 1994).

22. See Immanuel Maurice Wallerstein, *The End of the World as We Know It: Social Science for the Twenty-First Century* (Minneapolis: University of Minnesota Press, 1999).

the discrediting of the action of politicians as well as an increase in insensitivity to social injustices. The economy has become depoliticized. It is presented as a matter of mere technical administration, and the poor are made culpable for their own situation; they are accused of being maladapted to the new historical circumstances.[23] This context poses new questions for the theology of liberation as a theology of the political.

The Originality and Permanence
of the Theology of Liberation

It is appropriate here to ask about the originality and permanent content in the theology of liberation. Two elements should be offered in response to this question:

1. the method of "see, judge, act," which takes as its point of departure (material object) the social reality, critically interpreted, and struggles to transform this reality;
2. the preferential option for the poor.

With respect to the first point, one should recall that reality, which is never dissoluble from its interpretation, was radically altered after the fall of the Berlin Wall and the self-exhaustion of Fordism and in the crisis of modernity. The crisis in modernity brought with it the loss of plausibility of liberating historical projects that were gestated within modernity, an eventuality commonly called "the end of utopias." Positively speaking, forms of domination other than the economic were brought into consciousness, giving rise to a range of relatively autonomous liberation movements. These could not be integrated, and this led to the impossibility of designing a future ideal society that would conform to the situation of modernity. At the same time, these developments signify the end of one, single historical subject. This made possible the construction of history via a multiplicity of subjects, each bearing diverse claims and desires. The questions of gender, ethnicity,

---

23. See Slavoj Žižek, *Living in the End Times* (London: Verso, 2010); Christophe Dejours, *A banalização da injustiça social* (Rio de Janeiro: Getulio Vargas, 1999), originally published as *Souffrance en France: La banalisation de l'injustice sociale* (Paris: Seuil, 1998); Zygmunt Bauman, *In Search of Politics* (Stanford, CA: Stanford University Press, 1999); Antonio Baldassarre, *Globalizzazione contro democrazia* (Rome: Laterza, 2000).

and cultures took on enormous relevance, no longer reducible to the question of poverty, as was often the case in the past.

The loss of the capacity to imagine a precise design for the future coupled with disenchantment with the results achieved by politics led many militant Christians into a crisis of subjectivity. On its own, this crisis resurfaces positive dimensions by bringing into focus issues of personal happiness, affectivity, and desires, rescuing an entire field that has at times been repressed and negated. There also arose gratuitously a certain ludic dimension, one that furnished new possibilities for spiritual involvement and a more profound appreciation of the festive dimension of the faith.

At the same time, the question of serving the masses and of popular Catholicism has emerged in a new way. Increased religious diversity, the growth of Pentecostalism, and the rise of a group without religion even among the lower classes have raised new issues that present challenges for the theology of liberation and for the pastoral activity of Basic Ecclesial Communities. The crisis of modernity has had a profound impact in the field of religion, affecting the so-called historic churches in a manner different from the movement of modern secularization. This new process has generated new pastoral questions.

The changes do not really affect the fundamentals of the option for the poor built by the Latin American church, which lies at the very center of the theology of liberation. This option was recognized by the supreme Magisterium of the church as legitimate and necessary.[24] As such, the option for the poor is structural and structuring (*estrutural e estruturante*) for any form of Christianity; it can no longer be relegated to the level of other options of a circumstantial pastoral character. In the theology of liberation, the option for the poor gained two new particularly characteristic accents: the poor as an optic, or lens, for interpreting reality and the poor as an ecclesial and social subject. From its inception, a theology of liberation sought to be not a theology about the poor but rather a way of thinking derived from the social location of the poor. Here one encounters a whole gamut of questions that always accompany the debate over the theology of liberation, for example, questions about the possibility of having to be

---

24. *Sollicitudo rei socialis* #47; *Centesimus annus* #57.

dislocated from one's current social position. In some way, the theologians who produced a theology of liberation were always called to live in physical proximity to the poor, accompanying them in their lives and in their struggles, as a condition of the possibility of producing a theology from the standpoint of this social location. The social location of the theology of liberation was never that of the theologian as such, no matter how close he or she might have been to the poor.

One can also say that a theology of liberation takes the poor as its ecclesial subject and as the subject of its own destiny, that is, as an evangelizing agent capable of organizing itself and transforming the world and the church. In this sense, the dominant strand of the theology of liberation understands the poor to be a privileged historical subject that will bring about processes of social transformation, leaving behind every avant-garde or elitist perspective. Initially the theology of liberation identified "the poor" with rural laborers or with urban workers, the residents of the large outskirts or favelas where the Base Ecclesial Communities had taken shape. In the middle of the 1970s and through the course of the 1980s, as great changes took place in reality and in the way that we comprehended reality, we began also to include in the concept of "the poor" others who were then understood to belong to socially marginalized groups: women, blacks, and the indigenous. It was a vision of reality that still reduced the complexity of diverse oppressive situations to the economic category of "the poor." In other words, these persons were viewed primarily from an economic angle. Women, blacks, and the indigenous were the economically poor, that is, those whose fundamental situation, so defined, would on its own change into a new society that was economically and socially more just. Only in the 1990s would the autonomy and specificity of each subject and of the questions of gender, ethnicity, and cultures be rightly understood. Moreover, in that decade a new and urgent question came to be included in the discussion: the planet was already showing serious signals of ecological depletion. The prevailing economic system endangers not only the lives of the poor but all forms of life. The destiny of the earth and that of the poor are linked. Our future depends on ecological liberation and the liberation of the countless persons who are suffering under different forms of oppression, exclusion, and exploitation.

We thus arrive at the beginning of the twenty-first century. We can affirm that the theology of liberation remains timely and relevant, not in the repetition of a content worked out in the preceding decades but rather in the maintenance of the two fundamental principles that define it and permit continual reelaboration of its contents in order to respond to the questions continually posed to the Christian faith in Latin America. How can one be a Christian in a threatened world, in a continent with so many poor people who daily suffer various forms of oppression—sexist, cultural, gender, and ethnic? How can faith be proclaimed and witnessed in this context, and how can it be transformed into faith both believed and lived, capable of transforming our own lives as well as the world?

7

The Future of Political Theology

William T. Cavanaugh

When German theologian Johann Baptist Metz began writing on political matters from a theological point of view in the wake of the Second Vatican Council, he was among those paving the way for a new style of Christian witness, one that addressed the turmoil and suffering of the modern world in terms that were at once explicitly theological and at the same time took the political as the direct content of their reflection. Metz knew, however, that to label such reflections "political theology"—or the "new political theology"—was to risk grave misunderstanding. The term "political theology" had been coined in 1922 by Carl Schmitt in his book of the same name, subtitled *Four Chapters on the Concept of Sovereignty*. Schmitt was a Catholic jurist, not a theologian. Concerned about the instability of the Weimar Republic, Schmitt famously articulated a theory of sovereignty that placed the sovereign above the law in order that the sovereign be able to decide on states of exception to the law. Schmitt's ideas would provide some of the legal scaffolding for the rise of dictatorship in Germany, a rise that found Schmitt as the favored jurist of the Nazi regime until falling out with the party leadership in 1936. Though he lived until 1985, he was *persona non grata* in postwar West Germany. He spent a brief time in prison after the war and was never allowed to resume his academic post or receive a pension. For Metz in the 1960s to label his own work with the term most closely associated with Schmitt was a surprising and, some thought, ill-conceived move.

What looked ill-advised at the time now looks prescient. Schmitt is back. Now, however, it is not the right but the left—figures like Giorgio Agamben and Chantal Mouffe—that has found much of value in Schmitt's work.[1] At the same time, however, what Schmitt's interpreters mean by "political theology" differs significantly from what Metz and his successors mean. Political theology as Schmitt understood it is what he called "a sociology of juristic concepts,"[2] by which the formal structure of legal concepts such as state sovereignty and the state of exception are compared with theological concepts such as the sovereignty of God and divine intervention through miracles. By contrast, political theology as Metz understood it was theological in content, not just form. Political theology in this sense begins from the reality of God, whose will expressed through revelation serves as the basis of a critique of political orders.

The two concepts of political theology are thus different types of discourse that often talk past each other. In this brief paper I want to suggest what they can contribute to each other. From the Schmittian approach, political theology as done by theologians can learn to question the myths of secularization and disenchantment that often confine theologians' attempts to address the political. We can learn to take secularization less seriously, or rather, not assume that it is what it claims to be: the disenchantment of the modern world. From the Metzian approach, the successors of Schmitt can learn that the real reason that theology will not go away like it was supposed to is that, to put it bluntly, God has not gone away. True political witness can only be witness to the living God. I hope that what I mean by these cryptic comments will become clear as I proceed.

Political Theology of Content

Metz developed his political theology in the context of the 1960s, which was profoundly marked by crisis. War, nuclear tensions, racial issues, poverty, cultural upheavals, and more were met in the Catholic world by Vatican II's new attitude of openness to the world outside the church. The siege mentality of the previous century's *Syllabus of Errors* was replaced by the famous opening line of *Gaudium et spes*: "The joys and

---

1. Though Carl Schmitt has been positively invoked by some on the rightward side of the political spectrum; see Stephen H. Webb, *American Providence: A Nation with a Mission* (New York: Continuum, 2004), 153-66.

2. Carl Schmitt, *Political Theology: Four Chapters on the Concept of Sovereignty* (Chicago: University of Chicago Press, 2005), 37, passim.

the hopes, the griefs and the anxieties of the men of this age, especially those who are poor or in any way afflicted, these are the joys and hopes, the griefs and anxieties of the followers of Christ."[3] At the same time that the church was embracing the world, however, it seemed in many places that the world was rejecting the church. In Quebec, Belgium, and many other traditionally Catholic places, a rapid process of secularization appeared to be emptying the church into the world. Sociologists assumed that modernization and secularization went hand in hand, and so secularization took on an aura of inevitability.

Metz's political theology was in part an attempt to embrace secularity critically as the outworking of the gospel. The creation of a world of freedom outside of God and the kenosis of God in the incarnation of Jesus Christ are both movements in which God embraces the world and establishes it as having its own proper autonomy. God has handed over the world to human freedom. "Hence Christianity, as it understood more and more from its own origins, had to appear not as a growing divinization, but precisely as an increasing de-divinization and, in this case, a profanization of the world, dispelling magic and myth!"[4] For Metz, it was the medieval fusion of religious and secular, not the modern separation of the two, that represented the aberration from a Christian point of view: "Only because we tacitly made this impure medieval world view the model of the Christian concept of the world does the modern secularization of the world cause us religious difficulty. In truth, however, a genuinely Christian impulse is working itself out historically in this modern process of an increased secularization of the world."[5] This does not mean that Metz accepted the banishment of God from the world, or the modern idea of human maturity as the denial of the existence and relevance of God. It means rather that the world is autonomous from the church, and that the church's job is not to rule the world but to help accelerate the sweeping of the public space clean from myths and false idols. The church's role is essentially negative; Christian eschatology, according to Metz, shares with the progressive narrative of the Enlightenment a con-

---

3. Vatican II, "Pastoral Constitution on the Church in the Modern World (*Gaudium et spes*)," §1.

4. Johann Baptist Metz, *Theology of the World*, trans. William Glen-Doepel (New York: Seabury, 1969), 34.

5. Ibid., 35.

stant dissatisfaction with the present and straining forward toward the future. The Enlightenment in this sense is an outworking of the gospel, but rather than claiming to know more about what is to come, as secular ideologies such as Marxism do, the church's "eschatological proviso" claims to know less about what is to come, thereby relativizing and critiquing all attempts to claim that the absolute has been achieved in history.

The liberation theology that developed in the 1970s and 1980s was political theology in Metz's sense of interpreting and applying traditional theological loci such as Christology and eschatology in the context of political crisis. Liberation theology rejected Metz's pure *via negativa* for a more positive and utopian eschatology that looked for the kingdom of God to be realized, really if not completely, in the history of political struggle. Liberation theology in some of its early iterations accepted Metz's embrace of the Enlightenment narrative of the maturation of humanity and the autonomy of the secular. The treatment of the social sciences—often including Marxism—as real sciences essentially distinct from theology, akin to the hard sciences, was based on the idea that the world had its own relative autonomy and obeyed its own logic that did not require a theological lens to understand. As Clodovis Boff wrote in 1978,

> We touch upon the problem of secularization, which sets in relief the (relative) autonomy of earthly values. The notion is a legitimate one. Here theology would be incompetent to pronounce upon the internal regime of the [social] sciences. . . . Confronting the scientific process, theologians must wait, in an attitude of attention. They have nothing pertinent to say until they are correctly instructed as to what is transpiring "out there," at a distance from them.[6]

According to Boff, theology can critique social sciences if they exceed their limits, but within those limits they enjoy a definite autonomy.[7] It is not that God had abandoned the world to its own devices; it was rather that the world was imbued with God's grace and therefore

---

6. Clodovis Boff, *Theology and Praxis: Epistemological Foundations*, trans. Robert Barr (Maryknoll, NY: Orbis Books, 1987), 51-52.

7. Ibid., 52.

was not in need of deriving grace only through the mediation of the church or of theological reflection.

The first, most important, movement of both Metz and liberation theology was to turn toward the world outside the boundaries of the church and address theology to the political, social, and economic situation of the world. From the start, however, some Latin American liberation theologians, such as Gustavo Gutiérrez, while not questioning its relevance to the European context, questioned whether "secularization" applied to Latin America. In his discussion of Metz in *A Theology of Liberation* (1971), Gutiérrez wrote, "the universal existence of a secularized world and the privatization of the faith seem to have been taken for granted by political theology without further critical examination. Nevertheless, in places like Latin America, things are different. The process here does not have the characteristics it exhibits in Europe."[8] By the time that Gutiérrez wrote a new introduction to the revised edition of the book in 1988, he was at pains to distance himself from those who regarded liberation theology as a branch of European, Enlightenment-based theology,[9] and he explicitly repudiated views of the social sciences as autonomous: "we also know that the sciences and, for a number of reasons, the social sciences in particular, are not neutral. They carry with them ideological baggage requiring discernment. . . . In consequence, both the scientific outlook itself and the Christian conception of the world call for a rigor-

---

8. Gustavo Gutiérrez, *A Theology of Liberation: History, Politics, and Salvation*, rev. ed. (Maryknoll, NY: Orbis Books, 1988), 129.

9. "In the development of liberation theology our awareness of this new presence has made us aware that our partners in dialogue are the poor, those who are 'nonpersons'—that is, those who are not considered to be human beings with full rights, beginning with the right to life and to freedom in various spheres. Elsewhere, on the other hand, the best modern theology has been sensitive rather to the challenge posed by the mentality that asserted itself at the European Enlightenment; it is therefore responsive to the challenges posed by the nonbeliever or by Christians under the sway of modernity. The distinction between these two approaches is not an attempt to juxtapose two theological perspectives. It tries only to be clear on their respective starting points, to see their differences, and then correctly to define relationships between the two. If we follow this line, we will avoid yielding to a tendency found in some academic settings: the tendency to regard liberation theology as the radical, political wing of European progressive theology" (ibid., xxix).

ous discernment of scientific data—discernment, but not fear of the contributions of the human disciplines."

In the wake of the success of liberation theology, there has been a proliferation of theological reflections on the political, including postcolonial approaches, theological defenses of Christendom, theological explorations of the politics of gender, race, and sexual identity, church-centered approaches, public theologies of electoral politics, and a host of others. All of them have come to be grouped together under the rubric "political theology," from Hugo Assmann to Oliver O'Donovan, from Rosemary Radford Ruether to John Howard Yoder. Many continue to see their task as presenting a theological response to a secular world. What they have in common with one another and with Metz is an engagement with politics from a set of explicitly Christian theological commitments. (I leave to Muslims and Jews and others to decide whether "political theology" is a useful term in their contexts.) What has changed since the 1960s and 1970s, however, is that secularization is no longer universally regarded as a fact about the contemporary world, not only in Latin America but even in Europe, where church attendance and other indicators of Christian participation have fallen at an accelerating rate since the appearance of "political theology." Despite such indicators of "secularization," there is increasing talk of a postsecular world, and those who are considered postsecular often look to Carl Schmitt for inspiration. For it was Schmitt whose political theology opened up the possibility that what we tend to describe as secular—the world of law and politics and statecraft—is not autonomous from the theological at all, but rather deeply imbued with theological concepts borrowed from the church.

Political Theology of Form

There have been a number of factors that have led to the questioning of the secularization thesis that was once taken for granted. Former champions of the secularization thesis such as Peter Berger have now repented. Berger and friends refer to the "desecularization" of the world and the "resurgence" of religion in the latter decades of the twentieth century.[10] As evidence they offer the upswing in Muslim

---

10. Peter Berger, ed., *The Desecularization of the World: Resurgent Religion and World Politics* (Grand Rapids, MI: Eerdmans, 1999).

fundamentalism, the assertiveness of the Religious Right in U.S. politics, the continued growth of Pentecostalism and new religious movements in the West, the expansion of Christianity in the global South, the public visibility of Christianity in political struggles in Poland and Latin America, and so on. The end of the secularization hypothesis has now become a common trope, to be celebrated or lamented, but questioned by few.

It should be noted that the supposed "resurgence" of religion leaves the categories of religious and secular intact. There is, however, a more fundamental way in which these categories are themselves being questioned. Since the 1990s there has been a swelling of interest in the genealogies of the religious/secular distinction. Drawing on Wilfred Cantwell Smith's groundbreaking 1962 book *The Meaning and End of Religion*,[11] scholars like Jonathan Z. Smith, Talal Asad, Timothy Fitzgerald, and Daniel Dubuisson have shown that the religious/secular distinction is a modern Western invention and is not engraved in the nature of things. The most recent and comprehensive dissection of the concept of religion is Brent Nongbri's *Before Religion: A History of a Modern Concept*.[12] In a thorough review of the ancient and medieval terms that are commonly translated as "religion," Nongbri affirms the judgment of others that "religion" and the religious/secular divide is an invention of the modern West, subsequently exported to the rest of the world in the process of colonization. What counts as religion and what counts as secular in any given context depend on configurations of power. What this means for our present purposes is that there is no *essential* difference between religious and secular ideologies and institutions.[13] The secular is not an autonomous realm with its own logic, neither sewn into the lining of history by God nor the result of the emancipation of humanity from God. The secular can

---

11. Wilfred Cantwell Smith, *The Meaning and End of Religion* (New York: Macmillan, 1962).

12. Brent Nongbri, *Before Religion: A History of a Modern Concept* (New Haven: Yale University Press, 2012).

13. Of course, there remain those who try to rescue an essentialist definition of religion in terms of gods or the supernatural or some other characteristic that would separate out "religious" from "secular." I critique these views at length in my book *The Myth of Religious Violence: Secular Ideology and the Roots of Modern Conflict* (New York: Oxford University Press, 2009), esp. chap. 2.

be just as theological as the religious; nationalism's substitution of the nation for God does not turn it into something essentially different from what is commonly labeled "religion." This line of investigation takes its cue not from Max Weber, who wrote of the "disenchantment" (*Entzauberung*) of the modern world, but from Emile Durkheim, who saw that, far from being disenchanted, modern secular societies obey the same logic as supposedly more primitive or "religious" ones do. Religion is simply whatever binds a society together with taboos and borders separating the sacred and the profane. The flag of the modern secular nation-state functions in the same way that totems of God or gods function in nonsecular societies.[14] The sacred/profane distinction, in other words, does not track the religious/secular distinction.

Carl Schmitt's "sociology of juristic concepts" performs the same type of deconstruction of the religious/secular distinction. The legal structure of a "secular" state is not at all autonomous from theology; the modern theory of the state is not characterized by the relegation of God to a private "religious" sphere but by the translation of theological concepts into legal ones. The state acts as God did in medieval society; "the state acts in many disguises but always as the same invisible person," dispensing law, intervening in decisions, granting pardons, all with the same omnipotence "of which one reads in every textbook on public law."[15] This omnipotence, Schmitt argues, is borrowed not only in the linguistic sense from theology. Nor can the influence of theology on law be explained historically or psychologically. Theology is not reducible to material causes in the Marxist fashion, and material causes cannot be reduced to ideas. A proper sociology of juristic concepts is "a consistent thinking that is pushed into metaphysics and theology. The metaphysical image that a definite epoch forges of the world has the same structure as what the world immediately understands to be appropriate as a form of its political organization."[16] This is why Schmitt is not content to call his investigation "sociology" but labels it instead "political theology." The secular world operates on

---

14. See Emile Durkheim, *The Elementary Forms of Religious Life* (New York: Free Press, 1965), esp. chap. 1, where Durkheim considers and rejects definitions of religion restricted to "the supernatural" or to "gods" (39-50).

15. Schmitt, *Political Theology*, 38.

16. Ibid., 46.

theological principles, albeit disguised ones. It is in this sense that the followers of Schmitt today can be called postsecular.

Schmitt developed these ideas in the context of a critique of proceduralism in modern liberal states that tries to encompass all decision-making within the rule of law. Just as the sovereignty of God had been pushed aside by theories of the smooth functioning of natural laws, so political liberalism had tried to make the machine run by itself, in an entirely immanent and law-governed structure.[17] The liberal state tries to banish politics, that is, the art of decision-making, by appeal to law that eliminates the need for decision. One problem is that law will always be running to catch up with new circumstances and trying to cover over necessary exceptions to the law through the creation of more law. What is needed, according to Schmitt, is a concept of sovereignty in which the sovereign decides on the exception. The sovereign, while part of the judicial order, also stands above and outside the judicial order. Sovereignty, as Schmitt says, is a "borderline" concept.[18] This does not mean that exception applies only to occasional states of emergency. It is "a general concept in the theory of the state,"[19] which establishes the existence of a sovereign that transcends the merely immanent political process while it also constitutes that process. According to Schmitt, only something from beyond the system of law could make that system binding. There must be some authority from beyond law to make laws believable and obeyable.

The definition of sovereignty as a borderline case, something that straddles the immanent and the transcendent, is what makes Schmitt insist on the relevance of political theology. Attempts to reduce the state to a purely immanent process are futile; there is always a "theological" moment in any genuinely political process. Schmitt, then, allows for the possibility that the claims of the state to comprehensive competence and the view of the state as a closed—and therefore unquestionable and inescapable—immanent system can be challenged from a theological point of view.[20] What Schmitt means by a "soci-

---

17. Ibid., 48-50.

18. Ibid., 5.

19. Ibid.

20. On this point, see Ted A. Smith's excellent *Divine Violence: John Brown and the Limits of Ethics* (Palo Alto, CA: Stanford University Press, forthcoming), chap. 3.

ology of juristic concepts," furthermore, is not opposed to theology as discourse about God. In his discussion of this sociology, Schmitt writes, "Both the spiritualist explanation of material processes and the materialist explanation of spiritual phenomena seek causal relations. At first they construct a contrast between two spheres, and then they dissolve this contrast into nothing by reducing one to the other. This method must necessarily culminate in a caricature."[21] Schmitt was a serious Catholic, and did not think that God was a mere symbol invented by humans to correspond with merely immanent realities: "It is thus not a sociology of the concept of sovereignty when, for example, the monarchy of the seventeenth century is characterized as the real that is 'mirrored' in the Cartesian concept of God."[22]

Although he did not collapse sociology and theology in the ways that some of his successors have, Schmitt did have a tendency to collapse God into earthly sovereignty and see little if any practical distinction between God and the representatives of God's sovereignty on earth. For Schmitt, the crucial question of "Who decides?" can only be resolved in a practical way, short of the Lord's second coming, by appeal to concrete unitary state sovereignty. There could be no question of subordinating temporal to spiritual power.[23] The church's problem is that it tends toward the division of sovereignty within the social order, what Schmitt referred to as the "typically Judeo-Christian division of the original political unity."[24] Schmitt's solution is the practical identity of God and state.[25] From here it is not a long journey to viewing language of "God" as a metaphor for immanent social processes.

As we look toward the future of political theology, what can be gained from the study of Schmitt? Although Schmitt does not directly

---

21. Schmitt, *Political Theology*, 43.

22. Ibid., 45.

23. Ibid., 33-34.

24. Carl Schmitt, *The Leviathan in the State Theory of Thomas Hobbes: Meaning and Failure of a Political Symbol*, trans. George Schwab and Erna Hilfstein (Westport, CT: Greenwood Press, 1996), 10.

25. Passages like the following make it easy to see how Schmitt's successors find it easy to discard belief in a real God and to reduce God to a metaphor for political power: "Because state power is supreme, it possesses divine character. But its omnipotence is not at all divinely derived: It is a product of human work and comes about because of a 'covenant' entered into by man" (ibid., 33).

pursue the implications of his work, I think that part of the task of
political theology today is not only to expose the hidden theology
behind so-called secular forms of power, but also to ask what kinds of
political power are being established and reinforced by the disguising
of theological principles behind the veil of supposedly neutral and
autonomous secular discourses. What political theology can learn
from Schmitt is neither to embrace the secular world nor to reject
it, but to question whether there really is a secular world out there
devoid of gods and myths. There are, of course, secularity and secularism, but these exist as ideologies, not as simple facts. To perform
this kind of questioning is not at all to want to overcome the separation of church and state or to long for the reconstitution of a Con-
stantinian social order. It is rather to level the playing field between
theology and other disciplines. It is, more crucially, to enable the kind
of idolatry critique that the Bible enjoins on the followers of God. For
what Durkheim and Schmitt discovered in the twentieth century is
nothing more than a stock biblical theme: people worship all kinds
of things as if they were gods. A vital political theology today is one
that both sympathetically appreciates the inchoate search for God at
the heart of every human endeavor and critiques the idolatries that
do so much harm in our world, idolatries of nations and markets and
freedom and oil and material prosperity.

Because this type of idolatry critique depends on belief in one true
God, however, many of the successors of Durkheim and Schmitt are
unhappy with this trajectory of political theology. Yale law professor Paul Kahn, for example, has recently published a book entitled
Political Theology: Four New Chapters on the Concept of Sovereignty
in which he applies Schmitt's ideas to contemporary American juris-
prudence and the social imaginary. Kahn argues forcefully and per-
suasively that we can understand the American political and legal
order only by appeal to theological concepts such as sacrifice and
sovereignty. He asks how, for example, we can understand the world-
destroying threat of the American nuclear arsenal without appeal to
theological ideas, like world creation and eschatological destruction.[26]
Kahn argues that in times of war the president embodies the people

---

26. Paul W. Kahn, *Political Theology: Four New Chapters on the Concept of
Sovereignty* (New York: Columbia University Press, 2011), 11-12.

as Christ did in medieval imaginary.[27] Despite his plea to take political theology seriously, however, Kahn does not seem to have read anyone who would consider him- or herself a political theologian. What Kahn means by political theology begins with what Schmitt means by sociology of juristic concepts, but Kahn goes on to dismiss theology proper—that is, theology based on convictions about how God *really* is or is not—as impossible in the modern world. Christian political theology has nothing to do with what Kahn considers political theology: "The latter is an entirely secular field of inquiry, while the former expresses a sectarian endeavor that is no longer possible in the West."[28] Despite his Schmittian deconstruction of any essential difference between secular and religious discourse, Kahn nevertheless insists that his political theology is somehow "secular" and therefore reasonable and scientific in ways that "sectarian" political theology is not.

I think that the Schmittian type of political theology needs to learn from political theology that takes witness to God seriously. Kahn thinks that we have entered a world that is irreversibly past metaphysics. Metaphysics, he says, has been historicized, and "once historicized it is not a science at all but a rhetorical practice."[29] This is a typically postmodern move, one that sees all as flux. But in reality, this type of logic is not postmodern but hypermodern. It is simply the extension of capitalism, where all that is solid melts into thin air, as Marx put it. There can be no resistance to capitalist forms of oppression if there is no place to stand. So figures like Graham Ward have called for an end to the end of metaphysics. It is not simply that metaphysics can turn back the clock to resist the flux of hypermodernity. More to the point, the way that Kahn and others describe our current situation is simply empirically wrong. We do not live in a postmetaphysical, disenchanted world. As Ward says, "What is culturally evident is that although certain philosophers of both the analytical and the Continental traditions speak loudly about the postmetaphysical, contemporary living is shot through with metaphysical themes, desires, and dreams."[30] The exposure of the enchantment of the supposedly secular

---

27. Ibid., 86.

28. Ibid., 124.

29. Ibid., 116.

30. Graham Ward, *The Politics of Discipleship* (Grand Rapids, MI: Baker, 2009), 152.

world that Kahn undertakes so well should open the Schmittian type of political theology to the renewed possibility of metaphysics, not close that door for good.

There is no way to insist that Kahn and others recognize the existence and self-revelation of God. One would think, however, that the deconstruction of essentialist boundaries between religious and secular would open such scholarship to the possibility of theology. If we recognize the fact that the need to worship has not simply died away with the dying of Christendom but has mutated into other forms of worship, we might begin to wonder why human beings seem to be inescapably worshiping creatures. If the search for transcendence has not gone away, it may be because humans are hard-wired for transcendence, and if humans are hard-wired for transcendence, it may be that immanence is not all there is. The most economical explanation of the need to worship might be the existence of someone worth worshiping. Witnessing to this invisible God is the first and most important task of any political theology worthy of the name.

CHAPTER 8

Martyria: Witnessing, Interculturality, and Secularism

Peter Casarella

M*artyria* in the New Testament signifies an active way of bearing witness.[1] It is at least as personal as it is juridical, which leads to the likelihood that its true sense becomes lost in translation once we begin a conversation about Christian witnessing (at least in English). In certain cases, like those of Peter and Paul, this act of witnessing culminates in a martyr-like death. In English this is the more common semantic field for martyrology. *Martyria* in the New Testament thus includes the notion that words and bodies are intertwined in matters of life and death.[2]

In this essay I examine the contemporary significance of *martyria,* or witnessing. What are the life-and-death issues today that urge us to recall the testimony of witnesses? I would like to consider the meaning and significance of *martyria* in two contexts, that of intercultural dialogue and that of secularism. At first glance these two contexts seem quite separate, but on further inspection they converge.

There are two ways to recover the language of *martyria.* In the first instance, witnessing is the everyday struggle to hope for social reconciliation in the midst of violence and bloodshed born of tribalism. In the second instance, witnessing is an act of personal conscience that

---

1. See H. Strathmann, "μάρτυς," in *Theological Dictionary of the New Testament,* ed. Gerhard Kittel and Geoffrey W. Bromiley, vol. IV (Grand Rapids, MI: Eerdmans, 1967), 474-514, for these details and variations. One must include here its verbal variants (*martyrein, martyresthai*).

2. For more details about the biblical contexts, see my "Conversion and Witnessing: Intercultural Renewal in a World Church," *Catholic Theological Society of America Proceedings* 68 (2013): 1-17.

is oriented to an unshakeable truth about the inviolable moral worth of the human person. The first sense addresses the need for witnesses who seek reconciliation in the face of difference. The second sense addresses the need for witnesses who will show courage and moral steadfastness. These virtues pertain to all cultures and also to the relativizing challenge of secularization.

In what follows I will argue that social witness and witness to the truth of conscience are not separate contexts, even though the Catholic tradition has sometimes treated them as such.[3]

Martyria has a polyvalence in the world church that is often ignored.[4] We lose sight of this convergence when we look at witnesses and witnessing from just one part of the globe or from one end of an ideological spectrum. Furthermore, the necessary convergence of social witnessing and witnessing to the truth confirms the urgent need to expand the category of witnessing. In the past the category of testimony was often invoked to enact a quasi-empirical justification of the church's place in history. Bearing witness to cultural difference with the hope of reconciliation cannot be separated from bearing witness to the truth about God and the dignity of the human person in the face of secularism if we wish to hold on to the breadth and catholicity of the Christian category of witnessing.

The Ugly Wound of Beauty and the Cry of the Poor

One way in which these two senses of witnessing come together is through the vision of beauty. Beauty here is understood as a theological category that brings aesthetics and drama into a single domain. It is not the detached scrutiny of an art critic or professional museumgoer. The vision of sacred beauty is one that causes the viewer to

---

3. I am not denying that in different parts of the globe different emphases will rise to the fore. John Allen, for example, in *The Future Church* (New York: Doubleday, 2009), makes a solid argument for why the concern about secularism in Europe and North America does not carry the same weight in the global South. He also shows that the issues of social justice exist in the global South alongside a firm denunciation of moral relativism. My concern here is to show the polyvalence of *martyria* in and for the world church.

4. The phrase *Weltkirche* was given a decisive but still largely undefined impetus by Karl Rahner. See my discussion of this point in "Conversion and Witnessing," 3-4.

reflect on the raison-d'être of one's life. In this sense, beauty can and should wound the viewer.

Pope Benedict XVI, in a 2009 address delivered to artists in the Sistine Chapel, remarked about this transformative quality of beauty: "Indeed, an essential function of genuine beauty, as emphasized by Plato, is that it gives man a healthy 'shock,' it draws him out of himself, wrenches him away from resignation and from being content with the humdrum—it even makes him suffer, piercing him like a dart, but in so doing it 'reawakens' him, opening afresh the eyes of his heart and mind, giving him wings, carrying him aloft."[5]

In his apostolic exhortation "The Joy of the Gospel," Pope Francis commends the way of beauty with equal vigor:

> Every form of catechesis would do well to attend to the "way of beauty" (*via pulchritudinis*). Proclaiming Christ means showing that to believe in and to follow him is not only something right and true, but also something beautiful, capable of filling life with new splendour and profound joy, even in the midst of difficulties. . . . Each particular Church should encourage the use of the arts in evangelization, building on the treasures of the past but also drawing upon the wide variety of contemporary expressions so as to transmit the faith in a new "language of parables." We must be bold enough to discover new signs and new symbols, new flesh to embody and communicate the word, and different forms of beauty which are valued in different cultural settings, including those unconventional modes of beauty which may mean little to the evangelizers, yet prove particularly attractive for others.[6]

Like *martyria*, beauty is not a thing but a path to be followed by the disciples of the Lord. Beauty is what draws us closer to the Lord, whom we love in our hearts. Pope Francis includes the way of beauty in his commendation of missionary discipleship for the catechist

---

5. "You Are Custodians of the Beauty," address of Pope Benedict XVI of November 22, 2009, at http://www.zenit.org/article-27631?l=english. See also my essay "'A Healthy Shock': Tradition and the Epiphany of Beauty," in *Tradition and Innovation: A Study*, ed. Elisa Grimi (Cambridge: Cambridge Scholars, forthcoming).

6. *Evangelii gaudium* #167.

because one cannot bring people into the communion of the church with Christ at its center unless they are drawn to the Lord's beauty. The catechist is a custodian of beauty in a manner analogous to the artist. Pope Paul VI famously said, "Modern man listens more willingly to witnesses than to teachers, and if he does listen to teachers, it is because they are witnesses."[7] The "new language of parables" that Pope Francis commends in "The Joy of the Gospel" will certainly have to avail itself of creatively articulated, intercultural examples of witnessing, if it is going to play a role in the world church today.[8] Otherwise, relatively few will listen.

The attractiveness of beauty does not arise as a matter of efficacy or technique. There is an organic unity of beauty and justice. This point has also been a central concern of Latino/a theologians but also has plenty of other non-Latino adherents.[9] Cecilia Inés Avenatti de Palumbo has developed a Latin American reading of the wound of beauty that uses poetry and mysticism in the service of the wisdom of human woundedness.[10] I focus instead on the intersection of beauty and justice in the work of Roberto Goizueta and Michelle A. Gonzalez, two leading Latino/a theologians. Goizueta notes that an incarnational, sacramental faith is necessary to perceive the beauty of Christ in the practices of popular Catholicism and in the suffering of the poor. He writes about the tangibility of real symbolic presence in Latino Catholicism in terms of the relationship to God:

Ours is not a watchmaker God who creates the world, winds it up, and then withdraws into some separate spiritual abode,

---

7. Pope Paul VI, "Address to the Members of the *Consilium de Laicis*" (October 2, 1974), *Acta Apostolica Sedis* 66 (1974): 568, as cited in his encyclical *Evangelii nuntiandi* #41.

8. *Evangelii gaudium* #41.

9. Elsewhere I have written about the remarkable theology of beauty and justice in the work of Alejandro García-Rivera, especially in his *Community of the Beautiful*. See my essay "Beauty and the Little Stories of Holiness: What Alejandro García-Rivera Taught Me," *Diálogo* 16.2 (Fall 2013): 53-58, as well as Peter Casarella, "The Communion of Saints and Social Solidarity," *Concilium* 2013/3: 59-69.

10. Cecilia Inés Avenatti de Palumbo, *Caminos de espíritu y fuego: Mística, estética, y poesía* (Buenos Aires: Agape, 2011), esp. 125-77.

leaving us to fend for ourselves. God does not liberate us by leaving us alone. . . . For U.S. Hispanic Catholics, the crucified Christ, Our Lady of Guadalupe, Juan Diego, the saints, and all creation are the assurance that God is indeed here—not up in heaven or in some ethereal realm, but here in our very midst; they are the assurance that God is indeed real.[11]

This closeness to the divine becomes literally *in*tangible if submitted to a hermeneutic that is purely rational or even a romantic one that sees presence as a refraction of mere emotion. The poor see the oneness of their wounded bodies and the supposedly tasteless and unmodern gashes on Christ's side. Elitist modern gnosticism, Goizueta argues, wishes away the signs of the real presence in favor of a more sanitized Christ and a less wounded body.[12] Goizueta thus lays out the fusion of beauty and justice in terms of a Christian theory of perception.

Gonzalez builds upon Goizueta and concurs with his liberationist defense of seeing the form of beauty: "To deny the presence of theological aesthetics throughout the ages is to silence the marginalized voices of those who continued the tradition of seeing aesthetics as central to theological expression."[13] Gonzalez's point of departure is the highlighting of *lo cotidiano* ("the everyday") as a locus of theological expression in the gendered poetics of the Mexican nun Sor Juana Inés de la Cruz. From there she sees parallels with aesthetic turns in French feminism, the poetic theology of the Latin American Rubem A. Alves, and Alice Walker's novel *The Color Purple*. Each of these sources presents an alternative to the rather stark division between ethics and aesthetics that arises in modern Enlightenment thought (especially Kant). Gonzalez's central insight is that human ugliness is a constituent factor in the perception of the justice of divine beauty.[14] The normal human reaction to ugliness is to turn away. We do not think of the ugly as bearers of moral exemplarity. With the eyes of faith, those who gaze upon what is otherwise repulsive (e.g., the

---

11. Roberto S. Goizueta, *Christ Our Companion: Toward a Theological Aesthetics of Liberation* (Maryknoll, NY: Orbis Books, 2009), 82 and 84.

12. Ibid., 113-14.

13. Michelle A. González, *Sor Juana: Beauty and Justice in the Americas* (Maryknoll, NY: Orbis Books, 2003), 182.

14. Ibid., 183.

physically deformed, the grinding poverty of the poor) can see that God's chosen ones are "full of grace." The process does not end with an inactive gaze but with sacrificial acts of solidarity and the fitting complement of prophetic calls for justice.

The fusion of beauty and justice will not appear all at once. Such a reality never falls straight from the sky like manna from heaven. In fact, great patience is needed to see, judge, and act in the company of the poor. The late Ada-María Isasi-Díaz, who passed away on May 13, 2012, focused on this patient struggle for justice with her theology of *lo cotidiano*. Her *mujerista* account of justice is startlingly concrete. She argues on the basis of her engagement with and on behalf of Latinas seeking justice that they have understood central Christian texts "not in elaborated discourse but rather in thoughtful implementation."[15] The difference between the theory of justice of these two Cuban-American Catholic theologians is subtle but important. Alejandro García-Rivera holds firm to a vision of beauty and justice rooted in cultural difference. Isasi-Díaz sees the convergence of love and justice in the slow and patient process of social engagement at the level of the grassroots. She is not advocating thoughtless activism but rather highlighting the need for complementing theories of justice with practical wisdom regarding concrete implementation:

> A *mujerista* account of justice . . . has to announce our *proyecto histórico* in a precise enough way so as to make choosing necessary, so as to force an option against injustice and for justice.[16]

The problem with García-Rivera's cosmic liturgy of justice is that the solution seems to be present wherever you look. Isasi-Díaz sat with women who inherited practical wisdom and popular devotions from their mothers and grandmothers. What they offered in their simple stories—their accounts of how to arrive at *un poquito de justicia*—is the truth of the community's beauty.

---

15. "Un *poquito de justicia*—a Little Bit of Justice: A *Mujerista* Account of Justice," in *Hispanic/Latino Theology: Challenge and Promise*, ed. Ada María Isasi-Díaz and Fernando Segovia (Minneapolis: Augsburg, 1996), 325.

16. Ibid., 338.

Reinhold Schneider: Forging the Language
of Social Conscience in a Secular Age

I turn now to the second context, that of secularism. To portray witness to the truth in an age of secularism and relativism, I will begin with Reinhold Schneider. Hans Urs von Balthasar considered his stance so essential that he wrote a lengthy book about him in 1953 and then republished the work under the title *Nochmals: Reinhold Schneider* ("Back to R. Schneider") toward the end of his life.[17] Schneider was a poet and novelist who embodied the synthesis of theology and holiness that Balthasar thought was absent in the discourse of academic theology today. The original book from 1953 represents a historical and literary map of European cultural renewal. As Balthasar tells the story, Schneider was a seeker who read and re-read Kierkegaard, Schopenhauer, Nietzsche, and Unamuno and considered at one point in his life becoming Buddhist. His literary output was enormous; the Schneider bibliography appended to the 1991 edition of his book includes 164 book titles.

I will focus on two aspects of Schneider's witness: (1) his notion of a spiritual aristocracy, and (2) his opposition after 1945 to German rearmament. Schneider wrote about the coronation of emperors in the Middle Ages. He came from an aristocratic family. His father was a hotel owner in Baden-Baden. The family estate (Hotel Messner) was destroyed in 1956-57, which became an occasion for a profound sense of resignation and the occasion for the new last chapter in the second edition of Balthasar's book, "The Final Curtain." He idolized an idealized form of spiritual knighthood—whether it was found in the religious vocation of feudal knights, Shakespeare's self-renunciatory kings, or Bartolomé de Las Casas, whose defense of the Indians was the subject of one of his most popular books. Part of Schneider's interest in extending the category of an old world aristocracy to the saints of the twentieth century was to recover a vocabulary that deliberately repudiated the banality of bourgeois civilization. On this very point he cites Francis of Assisi, Ignatius of Loyola, and Cardinal Newman.[18]

---

17. The English title is very different: *Tragedy under Grace: Reinhold Schneider on the Experience of the West.*

18. Reinhold Schneider, *Tragedy under Grace: Reinhold Schneider on the Experience of the West* (San Francisco: Ignatius, 1977), 248.

In renouncing the colonial urge to amass power and wealth, he sees an underlying ethos that paradoxically has been lost but still needs to be restated so that it can play a role in society once again: "The knightly idea is open: Christian existence lives on the basis of mission and loses its raison d'être if it loses its mission: It is not 'the West' as a cultural area that is the ground that will bear us; but Western Christianity will bear us. Christianity is opened up for the world, for it must bear responsibility for the world." Schneider realized that systemic violence was written into the script of colonial expansion. The antidote lies not in sanitized histories that ignore the massacres or the Christian fortitude of a Las Casas. The challenge lies in marshalling "an equally unheard-of massing of Christian, supernatural powers."[19] Which Christian saints have been formed who witness to the self-renunciation in the individual soul and in the social body that can overcome this systemic corruption of the West? That is the question to which Schneider constantly returns, and that is why he still harbors a hope that some very democratic form of spiritual aristocracy could once again animate the Christian conscience.

Schneider opposed German rearmament but remained "selective and guarded" toward the end of his life with the label of pacifism.[20] Cheap pacifism that did not consider the consequences for the exercise of power in the face of genuine oppression Schneider considered "a No to life." "An entire people," he once said, "cannot be medical orderlies." In other words, he called the problem of peace "one of the most tragic problems of history."[21] He considered power to be indispensable in the construction of a state worthy of humanity and knew that the granting of power was inevitable, ambiguous, and dangerous. After the fall of Hitler, whom he adamantly opposed in writings that were carried by soldiers of the resistance into the battlefield, Schneider knew that his love for a spiritual crown had to be drastically rewritten. This "spiritual crown" becomes translated, according to Balthasar, into three words: freedom, conscience, and responsibility. Balthasar remains convinced of the catholicity of Schneider's mission to interiorize freedom, conscience, and responsibility—especially with an ethics that denounces violence in so radical a fashion.

---

19. Ibid., 249.
20. Ibid., 278-79.
21. Ibid.

Balthasar saw in Schneider the seed of resistance to secularism. The believer in living out this mandate is called to live it out with a courage that cannot be derived from the terms set by the world. Recourse to traditional formulas does little good in the light of the loneliness that the Christian faces in embodying this ethic of responsibility. One remains in communion with the church and through the church with the very heart of the world, but the personal anguish of the task is not thereby diminished.

Joseph Ratzinger/Pope Benedict XVI uses the category of witnessing to the truth in order to paint a broad canvas of how conscience and culture can be renewed in our times. Schneider is one of his heroes. Ratzinger's essay on this topic, "Das Gewissen in der Zeit" (literally "Conscience in Time," signifying in a noteworthy *double entendre* both "conscience in the historical tradition that has been handed on to us" and "conscience as a temporal process"), was published when he was a professor in Regensburg.[22] The essay treats the politics of a free conscience as developed in Schneider's influential novel about Bartolomé de Las Casas. Ratzinger deduces from the examples enumerated by Schneider that Christians do not gain power by revolutions. "Power," he maintains, "attains greatness when it lets itself be moved by conscience." Christians must struggle against totalitarianism (Hitler openly denied the free exercise of conscience, he recalls) and other ideologies that limit the freedom of conscience precisely in order to make space for the free play of justice. The cross of Christ bears witness to the fact that a powerless witness can make possible in a radical way the self-imposition of limits on the conscience of the powerful.[23]

---

22. Joseph Ratzinger, "Conscience in Its Time," in Joseph Ratzinger, *Church, Ecumenism, and Politics: New Essays in Ecclesiology* (New York: Crossroad, 1988), 165-79. The original is "Das Gewissen in der Zeit: Ein Vortrag vor der Reinhold-Schneider Gesellschaft," *Internationale katholische Zeitschrift "Communio"* 1 (1972): 432-42.

23. I also take up this question in "Culture and Conscience in the Thought of Joseph Ratzinger/Pope Benedict XVI," in *"God Is Love": Explorations in the Theology of Benedict XVI*, ed. John Cavadini (Notre Dame, IN: University of Notre Dame Press, 2012), 63-86. One key point is the address that Cardinal Ratzinger gave in Hong Kong in 1993, in which he stated: "A successful transformation [of the Christian message] is explained by the potential universality of all cultures made concrete in a given culture's assimilation of the other and its own internal

The recovery of Schneider was important for German Catholics and deserves a wider hearing, but it does not translate directly into an ethics for a world church. So let me conclude this section with some more general theses on the reasonableness of Christian testimony. The Catholic tradition places a certain amount of weight on the reasonableness of Christian testimony. The form of reason associated with testimony has sometimes been overly narrow in terms of an empirical proof or a Stoic defense of immutable laws of nature.[24] The texts just examined from myriad sources suggest ways in which the claim to reasonableness can be maintained while widening the domain of reason associated with testimony. The following four theses are hardly comprehensive. They are meant rather to demonstrate that the way of testimony can be pursued while avoiding the narrowing of reason or its elimination altogether in the name of a new voluntarism. The first thesis articulates the relationship between beauty and justice within the experience of discipleship. The next three theses conform roughly to the see, judge, act paradigm of the Belgian cardinal and founder of the Young Christian Workers' movement, Joseph Cardijn.[25]

First thesis: standing before a Christian witness, one experiences a free flow and interplay between the attractiveness of the witness (the piercing call of beauty) and the engagement in action (the pursuit of the good).

Second thesis (see): this movement from attraction to action (and vice versa) is part and parcel of the natural desire of the human person to see God. There is a humanistic path from beauty to action that has given inspiration to many Christians. Augustine's early love of Platonism and Simone Weil's path to goodness both exemplify this trajectory in different ways. But in the face of secularism, it becomes

---

transformation. Such a procedure can even lead to the resolution of the latent alienation of man from truth and himself which a culture may harbor." See Joseph Ratzinger, "Christ, Faith, and the Challenge of Cultures," Address to the Presidents of the Asian Bishops' Conference in Hong Kong during a March 2-5, 1993 meeting.

24. See Peter Casarella, "Conversion and Witnessing," 4-7.

25. Joseph Cardijn, "La formation des laïcs à leur apostolate," in Joseph Cardijn, *Laïcs en premières lignes* (Brussels: Editions universitaires, 1963), 151-73, here at 165. English: *Laymen* (sic) *into Action,* trans. Anne Heggier (London: Geoffrey Chapman, 1964), 134-58, here at 149.

particularly important to recognize that the movement from attraction to action takes place with the natural desire to see God. This stems from the goodness with which the creator has endowed the creature, which according to Catholic doctrine is never entirely displaced by the real presence of personal or social sin. To name this finality within the human and social rhythms of life becomes increasingly challenging in a culture that aims to bring all efforts to serve the common good into what Charles Taylor calls the immanent frame.

Third thesis (judge): since the natural desire is not fulfilled by our own efforts but by a divine act we need to articulate the gap that exists between what we hope to fulfill in listening to the testimony of a witness and what can be and will be fulfilled in the fullness of times. Maurice Blondel in his short treatise entitled *La logique de la vie morale* attempted to articulate this gap in terms of the always-present difference between the willed will (*volonté voulu*) and the willing will (*volonté voulante*).[26] There is a dynamism to human desire that exists on multiple planes and is never satiated by any one act in pursuit of the good. The gap can be bridged by God, and the presence of this gap does not lead to having the whole path of testimony being overtaken by a dialectical logic. Balthasar refers to the proper sense of the gap in terms of the *Unvordenklichkeit der Liebe*, the manner in which (divine) love has nothing that precedes it in the realm of thought. Zubiri, the teacher of Ignacio Ellacuría, utilizes the neologism "religation," from the Latin *religare*, to indicate the manner in which humans are "tied-back" or "re-connected" to the power of the real.[27] Commenting on this, Michael Lee writes,

> For Zubiri, "God" is not a concrete idea, "Being," or a "divine reality." As theologal, the term "God" signifies the scope of the ultimacy of the real. Thus, Zubiri weds discussion of the theologal to analysis of human reality and sentient intelligence.[28]

In Balthasar's case, we stand before unfathomable love and in Zubiri's case "reality . . . as a 'more' in the thing itself." Thus the gap is what

---

26. In addition, see also Hans Urs von Balthasar, "Liebeslogik" in *Theologik*, II (Einsiedeln: Johannes, 1985), 29-33.

27. Michael Lee, *Bearing the Weight of Salvation: The Soteriology of Ignacio Ellacuría* (New York: Crossroad, 2009), 54.

28. Ibid.

spurs us onward to come face to face with a God of unfathomable love. The more we learn about our own ignorance, the more we want to know. The presence of cultural diversity in the world church speaks volumes to the impossibility of fulfilling the gap. New forms of witnessing to Christ abound once one opens one's heart and mind to the richness of cultural diversity within the communion of faith.

The fourth thesis brings us to the third part of the triad of "see, judge, act." Ignacio Ellacuría spoke about this as *el encargarse de la realidad* ("taking charge of the weight of reality").[29] In my own words, I would like to start with the proposition that no action taken on the basis of following the example of a witness can circumvent the call to communion as an expression of social solidarity. There are two ways to understand this thesis, and both are important to understanding what is at stake. The first is to follow Pope John Paul II in "Ecclesia in America" and to recognize that social solidarity is the fruit of trinitarian communion. This means that the gift of communion makes possible the solidarity with the poor and marginalized in the church and through the witnessing character of the church in solidarity with and open to the entire world. The second way to understand this thesis is to consider the work of Truth Commissions and Holocaust survivors and others whose witness to the truth involves speaking truth to power. In other words, the gift of communion in this view promotes Isasi-Díaz's rightful admonition "to force an option against injustice and for justice."

Synthesis

How, finally, does a social witness converge with the testimony to the truth of conscience? We might be better off asking whether there is any authentic social witness that is not also based in a witness to the truth and vice versa. Latino/a theology provides the key of beauty as a path to justice. Schneider points to the personal act of self-renunciation. He paints conscience as something other than a beacon of light in the midst of darkness or a singular heroic action that grasps for the transformation of the entire world. He locates witnessing in the personal act of self-offering. In both cases we are confronted with the reality

---

29. Lee, *Bearing the Weight of Salvation*, 48.

that the beauty of conscience matures and ripens as it engages history. This is the hard lesson that the followers of Archbishop Oscar Romero had to see played out when he was assassinated in San Salvador.

Christ's preferential love for the poor is the watermark of authentic Catholic communion. Christ calls us to be disciples who preach the good news of social justice and peace. We cannot achieve this discipleship by attending only to the concerns of the individual. In the words that Pope Benedict XVI pronounced in Aparecida, Brazil, "'Love of God and love of neighbor have become one; in the least of the brethren we find Jesus himself, and in Jesus we find God' (*Deus caritas est*, 15). . . . The Christian life is not expressed solely in personal virtues, but also in social and political virtues."[30] If we recognize that we suffer together in the body of Christ, then we will also labor as part of our Christian discipleship to transform structures that perpetuate poverty and foment social strife.

Interpersonal and intercultural dialogue is essential in the diverse church. Effective and faithful witnesses to social reconciliation are desperately needed in our secular, privatizing culture. Pastors and scholars need to find new ways to collaborate in this project. Isasi-Díaz rightly emphasizes the everydayness of witnessing. The encounter with the person of Jesus Christ brings about a unique and always renewable change of heart. By allowing ourselves to encounter afresh the face of the Risen Lord, we make the church into a home and school of communion.[31] Encountering Christ can dissolve hardheartedness slowly, including the sins of racism and ethnocentrism. This encounter makes possible a new culture of hospitality. Welcoming the stranger gets to the very heart of what the Nazarene preached and taught in Galilee. The gift of a hospitable Catholicism remains our strength as a Christian community and as witnesses to a new reality in history.

---

30. Inaugural Session of the Fifth General Conference of the Bishops of Latin America and the Caribbean, Conference Hall, Shrine of Aparecida, May 13, 2007.

31. *Novo millennio ineunte* #16, 43.

9

Challenges and Opportunities for Testimony in a Secularized Culture

João Batista Libanio, S.J.

Here we have a really challenging theme. The secularized culture answers to the continents, to the countries, and to the regions. Certainly, secularization in Europe developed in a different way from in Latin America. I am going to speak from the Latin American context, so this reflection will have the color of my continent.

From the beginning, I would say that the two key words here are "testimony" and "secularization." As for the word "testimony," if we check its etymology, we will see that it comes from *testis*, which appears in English as "test." The word "test," as everyone understands, is used often in the academic world. One says that students must "take a test, an exam." So, in a certain way, testimony is an exam; the one giving testimony is placed in a situation and must show to others and to his or her self that which he or she wants to live and realize in his or her life. Thus, to give a testimony is to prove something; here it would be to give a testimony of faith. Living in a concrete situation, this means: if you see me, if you look at me, then you will see that in my behavior there is an element that reflects the Christian faith. This would be the sense of "testimony."

The word "secularization" requires a longer reflection because it is our central theme. There are many similar words to secularization. The Latin *saeculum*, which means something like "an age" in English, refers more to a span of time, say a century or one thousand years; but in Latin, when one says *saeculum*, one is talking about "world." So, the word *saeculum* is identical to the word "world," and the world may be thought of as "reality," *for all the centuries of the centuries*; it can be in time and it can be in space, and it is here that we are going to look at secularization, looking at time because it happens in a period of time, but affects a particular culture. Moreover, there are several words that seem to belong to the same semantic family and to have the same meaning of secularization, and thus we need to differentiate these words.

Much is said about laicization, for example, but it is not exactly the same thing as secularization. It is a term from French culture, of French context. "Lay" means that the person belongs to a society that can do without religion. So, laicization is the process through which the authorities of the culture want to exempt themselves, in a way, from the religious world. Thus, laicization has something of a sense of secularization, but in a very specific way. In other words, laicization refers to the autonomy of a secular world that does not want to be influenced by the religious world. In the Catholic Church one speaks, for example, about the laicization of a clergyman, of a religious man when he abandons his sacerdotal career and declares himself to be lay: here lay and *laicus* are the same word. So, laicization means that I leave the religious universe in which I have lived—the priesthood for example—and I go on to live as a lay person; and the same is true for the religious person in general. So this concept of laicization is frequently used in a religious context. When the process of laicization is taken to an extreme, we call it "laicism." In general, in English, the ending -ism means an extreme exaggeration of the concept: in the move from relative to relativism, "relative" is taken to an extreme; "laicity," when taken to an extreme becomes "laicism." In this sense, in speaking about laicism, I mean that in the process of laicization that which is "lay," or more properly, the lay person, goes to the extreme and wants to take any sign of religion out of his or her life. These are the two meanings of "laicization" and "laicism."

Similarly, we can also talk about "statism," which means that the state practically takes over the regency of the citizens and can do without any religious influence. So, I mean the following by statism: the state becomes the owner of the behaviors, the norms, and the rules, so that the people follow the laws that the state establishes; thus, there is a connection between laicization, laicism, and statism. Now, laicity is a more abstract issue.

Another similar issue, one already referred to as the way in which the religious person disappears, when this religious person is a Christian, is "dechristianization." The dechristianization of Europe, for example, means that the continent that was marked by Christian culture, by the Christian faith, by the Christian religion, by Christian religious practices, begins to abandon this Christian side. Here we may discuss the dechristianization of Europe that has a certain link to secularization, and that we will see little by little.

Another commonly used word is "scientism." It refers to an ideology, and thus, a way of perceiving or of interpreting reality by putting science as the major criterion of interpretation for all other realities. So, when we want to explain anything through science, we are imbued with a scientistic spirit because we can do without recourse to any other reality. For example, let us suppose that a religious authority invites a psychologist to examine a young man to see if he has an inclination to the religious calling. If the psychologist is one who respects the religious person, he/she is going to give feedback with an aim not in direct opposition to what a religious authority may offer and or what a religious person decides when he or she makes a religious decision. But if the psychologist is a scientistic person, he or she will say, "We can clearly understand the religious call from its psychological (and even biological) aspects as influences of certain endocrine glands, and so on," which is also a certain biologism. There is a strong tendency today to explain some affective reactions from pure biologism. I once read an article about a statistical study on love: when someone is in love, he or she has this many heart beatings, so many glands working ... in the article love was reduced to a simple biological aspect. If I want to explain love through the simple biological aspect, then, I am practicing scientism; if I want to explain religion through science, then I am practicing scientism in relation to religion.

Now, atheism is something else. Atheism means that even though I can be religious I do not accept that any superior phenomenon exists, in other words, what we call "God"— hence *a* + *theos*. *Theos* is "God" in Greek and *a* is the privative alpha. Thus, atheism can even accept a transcendence, as is the case of some atheists in Europe, like Comte-Sponville, who calls himself atheist, or Luc Ferry, too, but the transcendence is not the personal transcendence that we call God. It can be a transcendence that goes beyond the here and now, something much wider, but not God, and thus it is atheist. This is a way of showing that secularization can end up in atheism, but it is not identical.

When I talk about agnosticism, the case is a little bit different. In a certain sense I can live "without" God; I neither affirm nor do I deny God. I do not have the proof to either confirm or deny, so I stay, one might say, away from the question. Indifferentism has similar features. We talk much nowadays about how the young generation is "indifferent" and suffers from religious indifferentism. It means that the young look upon whatever is religious and say, "it does not interest me," or "I'm not connected to that." This is not exactly agnosticism because here we are not speaking about the existence of God, but we are saying that the religious world and God are irrelevant and have no importance to a person. In this way he or she is indifferent.

Now, let us turn to our real issue, which is secularization. We differentiate secularization from secularism. In general, in English, the ending -tion indicates movement. So secularization is a movement, and secularism would be secularization taken to an extreme. As I just mentioned, the ending -ism represents the extreme. So, secularism is secularization taken to an extreme.

Let us turn to the meaning of secularization. In order to understand secularization, I have to inquire against the background of what has been said about secularization. Here I use a distinction that can help us. It is the distinction between religion, religiosity, and faith. I think the phenomenon of secularization does not affect equally these three phenomena, which each have a certain different meaning, even while they are very connected to one another, having a relationship of imbrication. When I want to talk about religion, I refer to its institutional aspect, the aspect of organization. And what does religion organize? It organizes the relationship of the human being with the divine, with the transcendent, with mystery. But it also organizes the rites, doctrines, sagas, and myths; it has its books, it indicates what time to pray, it indicates the place, and it indicates those who are suitable for it. Organizing all these things is religion. It prescribes behaviors for people; it often binds people to a particular moral vision; it imposes moral norms, and it imposes ethical norms and behavior, but in its own name and not ethics as a purely philosophical reflection, and only as such behavior belongs to the religion. For example, that a woman wears a long dress covering her all the way down to her feet would be an element of the power of the religion. It has power as an institution; it has authority, and the people who adhere to it as their religion follow this power. So, looking at the word religion, I look primarily at its institutional aspect.

Now, when I talk about religiosity, I am looking at another aspect; I am looking at the subjective aspect of those practices that comfort me and that reflect my religious dimension: I like praying, or being at a particular place. Religion says: pray in church. Religiosity says: I pray wherever I want; I can pray in my bedroom; I can climb a beautiful mountain; I can climb the Andes and from there contemplate nature; or I can stay in a yoga position, contemplating. What am I satisfying here? I am satisfying my religiosity. It is a very strong dimension in all human beings. Were humanity to lose all its religion, it would become, in my view, much more animalized. And here there is a compliment to women: in general, women have a more developed religiosity, which is to be valued. This is why women are more religious. It does not mean that they follow a particular religion more closely, nor that they have more faith. Religiosity is expressed in practices, in exercises, and in rites, but as long as such rites are not imposed, in which case it is religion. But as long as religiosity is there it satisfies me. Religiosity, like aesthetics, is a human dimension that makes us happy and makes us fulfilled human beings.

Faith is another dimension that has a natural relationship with religion and religiosity. Now, the faith that I am going to talk about is the Christian faith, because each religion can talk about its own faith. The Christian religion, when it speaks of the Christian faith, resorts, above all, to the Holy Scriptures, to the revelation of the God-Father that throughout history has been explained, transmitted, and discussed in councils and documents, and it has a long tradition of this. The imbrication of the profound relation between Scripture and tradition constitutes the only and ultimate source of faith. Faith is the embracing of this great tradition that is Scripture, read, reread, transmitted, interpreted, and studied; and for the one who believes, it is what determines existence. I embrace it as the word of God and obey it, and in general faith is lived in a community. Thus, faith is communitarian and lived within a tradition.

Now we may examine the impact of secularization in relation to these three—religion, religiosity, and faith—and what testimonies we may give about it, and what are its challenges. First, it seems to me that for a given religion, secularization progressively diminishes the power of religion as an institution. Religion once guided and gave norms, and people used to follow these; but today ever increasingly religion loses strength in imposing its norms: people are autonomous; they are free. In political issues, the state takes charge of the decisions; in ethics, philosophy speaks; in other areas, psychology, sociology, and the sciences attempt to deal fully with human reality and do not want religion to adjudicate people's behavior. Thus, there is today a decline of religion as an institution that rules society. What rules society today is reason, and human reason is one of the strong characteristics of modernity; and in this sense modernity is highly secularizing in relation to religion, above all to religion as something public. So, religion realizes that it does not have to discuss many things in public, and it retreats to the private world, and there it guides those people who want to embrace it. So, religion grows in the private world and is reduced in the public world; and we call this movement secularization.

Another effect of secularization is the process of the desacralization of the world. Consecration (in the sense of making the world sacred) is still strong in Brazil. There is still much of the sacred and sacral, but secularization says "no" to the sacred, which many times is ignorant. For example, someone may be sick and ask for a blessing, as if the blessing could cure the disease. In other words, the blessing would be a sacred rite that the religion would use to cure a disease. Then comes the doctor who says, "No, I will be the one to cure the disease and I don't need the praying; I have the medicine, I have medication. . . ." So, in this sense, the loss of the sacrality of reality, of the gestures, and of the rites, is likely to grow. For example, there is the blessing of a car; there is a celebration in which people come and ask me to bless their driver's licenses or their new car. The world thinks that my blessing is going to prevent an accident, that God is going to protect the car, and that it will not be stolen. Since I am already a little secularized myself, I say, "Look, people, the blessing is not for the driver's license or for the car. The blessing is a call to responsibility for you, the driver, that you become responsible, follow the rules of the road, that you are careful in traffic." Then I reflect on it. They have come to me with a sacred world, and I respond to them with a more secularized world; but I appeal to faith so that they know that they are responsible before face of God and in face of the faith. Thus there is a tendency for this desacralization to also diminish.

Now a new thing that is happening in Brazil and in Latin America is that religion is becoming an object of study. Until recently, our civil governments did not recognize either theology as a subject or the theologian as a professional. A degree in theology as a civil study was not recognized by the government, let alone by the religions. Today these recognize it. Theology is one of the degrees recognized by the Brazilian government and is among the sciences. There is even a religious sciences degree. Moreover, the number of these degrees is growing quickly; there is a large demand, and there are a large number of colleges that are offering a degree in religious sciences. As for faith? The answer is no. One studies religion as one studies geography and history: one studies the founder, the history, and the myths, only through the scientific eyes of sociology, psychology, philosophy, or anthropology; in short, all these human sciences enter religion and begin to study it. I would term this the phenomenon of secularization.

Now we may turn to religiosity. With regard to religiosity, there is the interesting fact that secularization is producing an opposite effect: instead of reducing it, it is increasing it. Today's world is more religious than yesterday's world. It is impressive to see the religious forms that are emerging all over the world. Secularization produces a reduction of the strength of religion, but at the same times it adds to the strength of religiosity. This is why I want now to cover the most important issue to us, which is faith.

I have the impression that faith must look at secularization, considering both religion and religiosity, and realize that it should not be saddened that religion is losing strength. But faith must also be conscious that it possesses a new role in society. I believe that the main role of faith is to interpret behavior, human action, so that the Christian can live well. Faith does not need to be afraid of the phenomenon of secularization. It will also be a critic of religiosity. There are religious forms that run the risk of alienation; they run the risk of masking human liberty, of hiding human liberty. Christian faith is a faith that apostrophizes, hence the great challenge and the great opportunity: it challenges human liberty; it wants the human being to answer first before God, illuminated by the word of God, that he or she commits to the transformation of reality. The theology of liberation was a great lesson for all of us. We assumed very seriously all the challenges of the capitalist, bourgeois society under the light of faith, developing a critical reflection on the capitalist system not as economists, not as political scientists, but as people who believe in revelation. What are we going to work with there? Is it with the choice of God for the poor, with the teaching of Jesus, with the tradition of the church that privileges the poor throughout history? So it is these arguments that are going to move liberation theologians to criticize the system. Thus, it is not Marxism, or sociology, or socialism as such, even though we might see in these ideologies something consonant with the Christian faith; thus, it is revelation, it is the way in which God has acted in history. And from this way of God acting in history, we are going to act in the face of earthly realities, in the face of political realities, and in the face of economic, anthropological, and psychological realities.

So, faith brings a huge strength to the dialogue with all sciences. But this does not happen under the guise of "religious sciences," because these study in the name of science alone, whereas we, on the contrary, dialogue with other sciences in the name of faith. When, for example, a science wants to become absolute and to give the final answer, then faith comes and says, "There lies your limit. There is something, there is a bigger mystery; there is an action in God that does not fit inside your reflection." Thus, faith has a strength and a capacity as a critic that is very broad, and it does not accept any absolute that is not God.

As for the above terminology—laicism, dechristianization, and scientism—faith criticizes each of them because it perceives in these movements a kind of absolutization of the human being. We can say that the biggest sin of modernity is to make the human being absolute and infinite. But when modernity is a critic, it joins a dialogue with Christianity and with the Christian faith, and it realizes that human reason is capable of discovering values; but it is not the last criterion of truth. All human truths fall under the judgment of God. And this is the most important function of the Christian faith, and I would say that it is also its greatest opportunity. The more the world becomes secular, the more religion is reduced in strength. Religiosity provokes modifications that are opposed to growth; faith, in a certain way, remains in a particular balance. It looks at the other two (secularism and religiosity) and accepts neither the extreme of religiosity nor the silence of a purely privatized religion. Faith has a public character as well. A famous theologian, Johann Baptist Metz, defended political theology and the church as a critical instance of society. He said that the Christian faith has the opportunity, the chance to face the challenges of modernity in a critical way, coming from what it is—in other words, the consciousness of faith itself.

Another important thing that faith can do is to dialogue with the freedom of religion. Religions are emerging from all corners, and this can lead us to a certain relativism, as if all religions were equal. Faith will say that all religions are true, but they are not equally true. Faith is able to help us differentiate here, even within our own Christian religion, how to live the faith institutionally. It will do this even for our way of living our Christian religious practices, which are the way of giving religious form to the faith that falls under faith's criticism. Faith is self-critical in the face of these religious forms and of the Christian religion itself. Christian faith, for example, is very critical in the face of ecclesiastical authoritarianism, that is, of certain ecclesiastical institutions that impinge on its role.

So, Christian faith has a chance, now more than ever. Secularization is the crisis of religion; but it is also the explosion of religiosity, and it allows for a more and more lucid faith.

10

The Symbolic Witnessing of the *Tinkunaco* Rite: Prophecy, Politics, and Popular Latin American Wisdom

Juan Carlos Scannone, S.J.

The current discussion comes from the conference "Witnessing: Prophecy, Politics, and Wisdom." For that reason, I choose here to focus on the *Tinkunaco*[1] rite because it constitutes a *witnessing* of popular Latin American wisdom, a type of political theology in symbolic action, one, which, if interpreted properly, implies a strong *prophetic* content and a robust *ethical-political* questioning. In addition, this rite, practiced annually in the Argentinean city and province of La Rioja, is closely connected to the blood witness of Monsignor Enrique Angelelli. The bishop of La Rioja, Angelelli celebrated the *Tinkunaco*, interpreting it in his sermons in the light of liberation theology. In 1967, after the burial of two other martyr priests—one of whom, Fr. Carlos Murias, a Franciscan friar, was my student at San Miguel—Monsignor Angelelli was murdered by the military. Thus, the memories of those Riojan martyrs can also be used to commemorate the UCA (Universidad Centroamericana) martyrs of El Salvador, among whom we can count two of my fellow theology colleagues in Innsbruck: Ignacio Ellacuría and Segundo Montes.

First, I will describe the *Tinkunaco* rite. Second, I will interpret its sapiential, symbolic meaning and its prophetic-political value. Third,

---

1. I restate and complete what was published in my book *Evangelización, cultura y teología* (Buenos Aires: Guadalupe, 1990; 2d ed., Buenos Aires: Guadalupe, 2011), appendix to chap. 12.

I will suggest a different line of thought concerning the cultural *mestizaje*, the new fruit of the conflictive encounter that the *Tinkunaco* ritually represents. Finally, I will warn about the danger of letting the rite remain a *mere ritual and symbol*, with no historical validity or political bite. At the same time, I will point out the intrinsic dynamism it contains so that we can move to a genuine, effective practice of the rite, that which impelled Monsignor Angelelli—and so many others—to the act of witnessing, not just in word but also in deed, through the shedding of blood.

The *Tinkunaco*: Symbolic Encounter
of Two Peoples and Cultures

Every year, on December 31 at noon, the people of La Rioja—a northwestern Argentinean province—celebrate the popular festival *Tinkunaco*,[2] a Quechua word that means "encounter." The festival is the symbolic celebration and ritual of conflictive encounter and reconciliation between two nations, two races, two cultures—namely, the Spanish and the indigenous—that today form one single *mestizo* people which is the common product of both. Using the Puebla Document of the Second Conference of the Latin American Episcopate, it can also refer to the "cultural and racial *mestizaje*" (*Puebla Document* 409),[3] the result

---

2. About this popular celebration see J. C. Vera Vallejo, *Las fiestas de San Nicolás en La Rioja*, 4th ed. (La Rioja: Talleres de la Imprenta del estado, 1970); J. Cáceres Freyre, *El encuentro o Tincunaco: Las fiestas religiosas tradicionales de San Nicolás de bari y el Niño Alcalde en la ciudad de La Rioja* (Buenos Aires: Instituto Nacional de Antropología, 1967); B. Jacovella, *Fiestas tradicionales argentinas* (Buenos Aires: Lajouane, 1953). In literature, the Tinkunaco is described by the Riojan Joaquín V. González in his book *Mis montañas*, ed. A. Marasso (Buenos Aires: Ediciones Estrata, 1958).

3. For the document in Spanish, see http://www.celam.org/conferencias/Documento_Conclusivo_Puebla.pdf. The category *mestizaje* is used also philosophically; see chap. 10 ("'Mestizaje cultural': Categoría teórica fecunda para interpretar la realidad latinoamericana") of my book *Nuevo punto de partida en la filosofía latinoamericana* (Buenos Aires: Guadalupe, 1990; 2d ed., 2011); also found in S. Montesino, "Mestizaje," in *Pensamiento crítico latinoamericano: Conceptos fundamentales*, II, coord. R. Salas Astrain (Santiago: Universidad Católica de Santiago, 2003], 655-62; C. Cullen, "El *éthos* barroco: Ensayo de definición de la cultura latinoamericana a través de un concepto sapiencial," in *Racionalidad técnica y cultura latinoamericana: Ponencias y comunicaciones.*

not only of the conquest dialectic (master/slave), but also the dialogue of encounter: man/woman.

The symbol of such encounter is that of two images (or, better said, of the processions that bear them): one of St. Nicholas (patron saint of La Rioja) and the other of the "Mayor Child Jesus." The former procession starts from the cathedral and the latter from the Church of Saint Francis. From opposite directions, they converge in front of the province capitol building, the *Casa del Gobierno* (formerly, in front of the town council), on New Year's Eve, when, according to tradition, the new mayor would assume office in colonial times.

The procession bearing the statue of St. Nicholas is presided over by the *alférez* ("second lieutenant," or "flag bearer"—in Spanish colonial times, the *alférez* carried the royal banner). The *cofrades* (lay members of a *cofradía*, a religious brotherhood) who accompany the statue— and who have arrived on horseback—wear a purple sash across their chests (the bishop's purple of St. Nicholas) and carry in their hands a flagpole bearing a multicolored flag. Through all of these symbols, including the *alférez*, the *cofrades* represent the Spaniards.

The other procession bears the Child Jesus clothed in the traditional dress of a town mayor (including the typical mayoral feather hat and either the pocket watch or ceremonial staff). Leading this procession is the *Inca*, emperor of the Incan Empire and symbol of the native indigenous people. Accordingly, the *cofrades* who accompany the *Inca* wear white headbands and, over their chests and backs, a type of scapular of small mirrors. An arch decorated with multicolored hanging ribbons is waved over the *Inca's* head, as if dancing to the beat of the bass drum. At the same time, in honor of the Holy Child and his Mother, the *Tinkunaco* song is sung in the Quechua language, the common language of the Incan Empire, a language that no one in the modern-day procession speaks or understands.

At the precise moment of the encounter, under La Rioja's burning midday summer sun, an absolute silence reigns. There and then, all those in attendance kneel three times before the Child Jesus, recog-

---

Tercer seminario internacional interdisciplinar del Intercambio Cultural Alemán-Latinoamericano, Santiago de Chile 23.7.1981–29.7.1981, ed. P. Hünermann (Santiago: Casa de Ejercicios de Bellavista, 1982), 10-36; see a critical view in S. Castro Gómez, *Crítica de la razón latinoamericana*, 2d ed. (Bogota: Pontificia Universidad Javeriana, 2011), chap. 3.

nizing him as mayor of the town, the province, and the world. Held by those representing the indigenous, the Child Jesus is also reverenced by St. Nicholas, who also seems to kneel as those representing the Spaniards genuflect under the platform on which they carry him.

An ancient legend tells the origin of the *Tinkunaco* rite. It is said that, in colonial times, there was a rebellion by the indigenous because of the injustices the Spanish mayor committed against them.[4] The rebels threatened to destroy La Rioja. While the Spaniards surrendered to prayers and penitence, begging God for the salvation of the town, St. Francis Solano, a Franciscan missionary (perhaps playing his famous violin), walked unarmed toward the rebels to pacify them. The rebels, in response to his preaching, accepted baptism by the thousands. The condition for reconciliation was the removal of the unjust mayor. And since then, all Riojans—whether descendants of Spaniards and/or the indigenous—recognize the Child Jesus as the town's mayor to ensure that justice is exercised in La Rioja. Even to this day, the governor of the province—the highest authority in La Rioja—accepts at that moment the Mayor *Niño*'s sovereign authority and surrenders to him the keys to the city. With this action, he recognizes that he governs on behalf of the Mayor *Niño* and should do so according to the Child Jesus' spirit of peace and justice, above all toward those who are the weakest.

A Political Theology in Symbols

Symbolically representing the origin of the Riojan people, the rite and the legend make them newly aware of themselves as the unique product of the conflictive encounter of two nations, races, and cultures: a fruitful *mestizaje*. Powerful, lifelike representations, those symbols also question injustice and inequality. However, rather than intensifying or worsening the conflicts, their symbolic potential instead promotes reconciliation based on justice, law, and personal encounter.

---

4. See the historical data and legendary aspects in L. Plandolit, *El apóstol de América: San Francisco Solano* (Madrid: Cisneros, 1963) (with bibliography and works cited); see also N. Rivera, *La Rioja: Su origen y tradición* (Buenos Aires: López, 1959). Many oral and written versions of the legend exist, but we cannot compare them critically to one another here. The rebellion by the indigenous and their conversion by Saint Francisco Solano are historical.

.

Both the rite and the legend tacitly demand, through their symbols, a just social peace in which preference is given to the poorest and most oppressed, those who gather beside the Mayor *Niño*. In addition, the *Tinkunaco* symbolically confesses that all political authority comes from God and must be exercised for the common good, with special care for those who are victims of injustice.

Christ is Lord and mayor, but he is also a child who loves with a special preference the "small ones," those who hold him as their patron and symbol. He is the peacemaker who achieves reconciliation between those who, repenting, recognize his just and gentle authority. That is why the *Tinkunaco* can be considered a "political theology" structured in symbols, rite, and legend. It is a political theology celebrated each year, and each year it is brought again to memory, re-presented ritually, and in that way proclaimed as well. At the same time, the *Tinkunaco* implies the witnessing/testimony of a seminal event, a political invitation to understand what it means, a prophetic denunciation of what opposes it within current society, and a declaration of political potentialities that challenge our freedom to make them real and effective.

For Paul Ricoeur, symbols communicate not only meaning but also truth, as soon as they reveal and expose, metaphorically, the deepest *reality* and the most proper *real possibilities*.[5] If Ricoeur is correct, the *Tinkunaco*—as perceived by popular religious wisdom—is then the ritual expression of the deepest historical identity of the Riojan people (and perhaps, by extension, of all Latin American people). At the same time, it is a living symbol not only of their deep longing for justice and peace but also of the real possibilities they hold within to effectively carry out, in history, the encounter with God and among humanity. Furthermore, it is a protest, in the form of a living representation, against any possible injustice or breach of peace.

Repeated every year, the rite is a new call each time to bring about those real possibilities in historical praxis. It reflects the origin and the most intimate historical identity of a people who are the fruit of encounter and *mestizaje*, despite the conflicts that were, and are, part

---

5. See his work *La métaphore vive* (París: Seuil, 1975), especially the seventh and eighth studies. See also chap. 13 ("Simbolismo religioso y pensamiento filosófico según Paul Ricoeur") of my book, previously cited, *Nuevo punto de partida en la filosofía latinoamericana*.

of their story. As I stated earlier, in and of itself, the man-woman dialectic—without dismissing the cruelty of the master-slave dialectic—nevertheless, calls for and results in, an overcoming of this cruelty through a new, unique fruit: cultural *mestizaje* and, quite often, racial *mestizaje* as well.

Cultural *Mestizaje* and the Vindication of the Oppressed Mother

In the view of Uruguayan thinker Alberto Methol Ferré, two of the dialectics that, according to St. Paul, were reconciled in and by Christ, were the man-woman and the master-slave dialectics. These, as theorized by Gaston Fessard, were intertwined and made fruitful in the origins of Latin America. In Latin America, the racial and cultural *mestizaje* of the man-woman dialectic predominated over extermination of the indigenous—the latter of which was the case in other regions—even though such *mestizaje* was indeed marked by *master-man/woman-slave* domination and oppression.[6]

In later interpretations of Latin American *mestizaje*, the ideology of cultural "whitening" sometimes prevailed, as in the novel *Doña Barbara*, written by Venezuelan Rómulo Gallegos. In the novel, Doña Barbara is a *mestizo* character, who, as her name indicates, poetically represents *barbarie* (barbarism), in the sense the Argentinean author Domingo F. Sarmiento gives this word in the subtitle of his own work, *Facundo*. There, when he talks about civilization and barbarism, the latter is understood as the opposite, the antithesis, of Western civilization. In contrast to the character Doña Barbara, her daughter must westernize and "whiten" herself to be able to marry Santos Luzardo, whose first and last name evoke, respectively, Christian sanctity (*santos*) and the light (*luz*) of modern enlightenment.

In contrast, in recent times, the culture of the mother—especially the indigenous mother—is being reclaimed, as in the figure of the indigenous Rendón Wilka in the novel *Todas las sangres* by José María

---

6. See A. Methol Ferré, "Análisis de las raíces de la evangelización latinoamericana," *Stromata* 33 (1977): 93-112; it employs writings from G. Fessard, "Esquisse du mystère de la société et de la histoire," *Recherches de science religieuse* 35 (1948): 5-54, 161-225, and G. Fessard, *De l'actualité historique* I (París: Desclée de Brouwer, 1960).

Arguedas. A cultural *mestizo*, Wilka in some way brings together in himself a balanced synthesis of all the races and cultures of Peru. It is no coincidence that he is greatly appreciated by fellow countryman Gustavo Gutiérrez, the father of liberation theology. What Wilka and other Arguedas's characters poetically symbolize is something that is currently happening socially and culturally in the popular suburban culture of our larger Latin American cities. A new *mestizaje* of cultural imaginaries is occurring, which seems to foreshadow the path toward a genuine and liberating interculturality. This new *mestizaje* is about a new living synthesis, similar to what was described in the Puebla Conference (*Puebla Document* 448): a synthesis not only between the cultures of different ethnicities but also between the values and symbols of the traditional cultures and the values and symbols of modern and postmodern cultures.[7] Consequently, emerging today there is a true challenge to Latin American politics and the pastoral approach to culture(s), both singular and plural. And this is also a challenge to Latin American liberation theology.

In addition to the two human dialectics of man-woman and master-slave, St. Paul also takes into consideration a theological one: Jew-Gentile, a dialectic also analyzed by Fessard. If we apply these three dialectics to the first evangelization of the Americas, we find that the oppressed indigenous woman, mother of the first racial and cultural *mestizaje*, in effect converted herself from gentile/pagan to Christian, the mother of Christian children. And we also find that, regarding the Iberian male slave master, a contradictory ambiguity developed that was harshly criticized by many priests beginning with Bartolomé de Las Casas. Through evangelization and baptism, the dignity of the converted pagans was recognized and, implicitly, the dignity of their cultures as well. Yet, on the other hand, they were

---

7. See P. Trigo, *La cultura del barrio* (Caracas: Universidad Católica Andrés Bello, 2004); P. Trigo, *Cómo relacionarnos humanizadoramente: Relaciones humanas entre personas y en la sociedad* (Caracas: Centro Gumilla, 2012); J. Seibold, "Imaginario social, religiosidad popular y transformación educativa," in *Argentina, tiempo de cambios*, ed. D. García Delgado et al. (Buenos Aires: San Pablo, 1996), 323-47; J. Seibold, "Ciudadanía, transformación educativa e imaginario social urbano," in *Lo político en América Latina: Contribución filosófica a un nuevo modo de hacer política*, compiled by J. C. Scannone and V. Santuc (Buenos Aires: Bonum, 1999), 463-511.

not in actual fact recognized for their value as part of humanity, as if somehow the indigenous people were not culturally or politically adults. And this was the line of reasoning used to justify, ideologically, the conquest and the *encomienda* system.

The symbology of the *Tinkunaco* not only reevaluates the cultural *mestizaje*, renewed today by the new *mestizaje*—traditional, modern, and postmodern—of cultural imaginaries in the suburbs of large Latin American cities, it also, without forgetting the "father's" inheritance, preferably restores that of the "mother" as well. The *Tinkunaco* symbology not only brings together the existential, human, and religious wisdom of the *buen vivir*[8] of the original indigenous people (above all, those who were evangelized), but it also unites into a new living synthesis the wisdom of the *mestizo* with the contributions of Western science and technology to achieve a more humane, equitable, and just society. Pedro Trigo's proposal of a *"pluricultural* Latin America which proactively contributes to an *alternative globalization"*[9] is already being practiced in more than a few emerging areas in suburban cultures, for example, of greater Buenos Aires. I prefer, however, to speak of this as interculturalism. Among other examples, I think of the *cartoneros* (garbage collectors) of suburban Buenos Aires, who, thanks to the intervention of church officials, learned how to recycle plastics from scientists and technicians at the Universidad Tecnológica Nacional de Quilmes. This enabled them to free themselves of the middlemen who were exploiting them. The *cartoneros* embraced the contributions of modern science, combining them (I would say *mestizándolos*) with their own popular, entrepreneurial, creative, and solidarity-engendering wisdom.

Ambiguity and the Power of Symbols

It is clear that, given their plurality of meanings, symbols such as those of the *Tinkunaco* rite can also be ideologically manipulated in order to disguise oppression and thus limit justice, conversion, and

---

8. A formula that somehow is repeated in different indigenous cultures: *allin kausay* in Quechua; *sumak quamaná* in Aymara; *tokó porá* in Guaraní. It means to live in harmony with oneself, others, the earth, and God.

9. See Trigo's statement in chap. 6 of *Cómo relacionarnos humanizadoramente*: "Construir una América Latina pluricultural para contribuir proactivamente a una globalización alternativa."

reconciliation *only* to the religious and symbolic level, without any ethical, political, and social effectiveness. But doing so would be to restrain the internal dynamism that belongs to them as symbols and betray the truth that they metaphorically present and proclaim.

In contrast, an authentic theology of liberation and evangelization of the culture can, with the Word of God, illuminate the popular, human, and Christian wisdom shaped in those symbols, so that they can be theologically interpreted and put effectively into practice. In the same way, those symbols and their human interpretation can serve as instruments for an acculturated understanding of this very same Word of God and its message of reconciliation, peace, and justice in Christ.

As already implied, we can find important guiding principles for a theological and pastoral interpretation of the *Tinkunaco* in terms of liberation and in the light of the gospel in the pastoral writings, preaching, and actions of one of the most prominent Riojan priests: the previously mentioned Monsignor Angelelli, who was martyred for his defense of justice and human rights. The beginning of the process for his beatification confirms him as a model for all.

Consequently, the *Tinkunaco* seems to be the ritual fruit of the evangelization of the culture, shaped in symbols of popular devotion. The human and Christian wisdom that they express can serve as mediator for an acculturated theology that takes the religious symbols of a people seriously and illuminates, interprets, and discerns them in the light of the Word of God. These can also serve, especially, as mediator of a political theology that prophetically denounces the social inequality that exists today in Latin America and can politically invite, or move, our freedom to make a more humane and just society a reality.

11

Memory, Mysticism, and Testimony

J. Matthew Ashley

Introduction

The link between memory and testimony—particularly in its meaning as "bearing witness"—seems clear enough. One must remember in order to give testimony, and remember correctly in order to give testimony reliably. By intercalating a third term—"mysticism"—my intent is to explore a mystical transformation that is, I think, evident in the martyrs of El Salvador, and exigent on those who would carry on their memory. The goal of this brief reconnaissance is to show that one element of the link between correct memory and reliable testimony is a particular mystical stance on the part of the one who forges this connection in her or his life. In the course of this exploration I assume without arguing the insistence in recent scholarship on Christian spirituality that "mysticism" is not best detected and measured by the occurrence of supernatural visions or preternatural experiences of self-annihilation, but rather marks a transformation of the person as a whole. For Christian mysticism in particular, this is a transformation that makes one more able to love. Moreover, I take a hint from a tradition, going back at least to Augustine, but continued in the Middle Ages, that defines the human soul—human subjectivity, if you will—in terms of the interwoven powers of reason, will, and memory. There was a lively debate in the high and late Middle Ages over whether union with God that represents the heart and goal of the *vita contemplativa* had its epicenter in the intellect or in the will—with the Dominicans more or less aligning with the former opinion and the Franciscans the latter. No one, to my knowledge, ever explored at length the possibility that memory might be a locus of mystical union, even though memory was held in high esteem in the

Middle Ages.[1] Following this hint I would also describe my foray here as something of an experiment. Are there gains to be had from thinking about mystical union as something like a "union of memories," a transformation of memory that then contributes to the witness of love, to testimony? Might this way of thinking help us to appreciate and to learn from martyrs such as Rutilio Grande, Oscar Romero, Ita Ford, and Ignacio Ellacuría?

I proceed in three stages. First, no progress can be made as long as one sees in memory only the cybernetic recall of facts from the past. Only defining memory more broadly makes of it a genuinely theological category. For this redefinition of memory I draw on Johann Baptist Metz, who drew for his part on the work of Walter Benjamin and Herbert Marcuse. Second, if we are to think of a "union" of memories," we must also think—with all necessary analogical caveats—about God's memory. For this I draw on the thought of Gustavo Gutiérrez. In bringing their conceptions of memory into conversation I then draw out two implications for the theme of this volume related to what I will call an "anamnestic mysticism."

Johann Baptist Metz: Anamnestic Reason and the Dialectic of Remembering and Forgetting

Catholic theologian Johann Baptist Metz adopted memory as a key anthropological and theological category in the late 1960s, under the decisive influence of Walter Benjamin, so we begin with Benjamin. In one of his "theses on the philosophy of history," Benjamin wrote the following:

> We know that the Jews were prohibited from investigating the future. The Torah and the prayers instruct them in remembering, however. . . . This does not imply . . . that for the Jews the future turned into homogeneous, empty time. For every second of time was the strait gate through which the Messiah might enter.[2]

---

1. On the importance of memory I rely on Mary Carruthers, *The Book of Memory: A Study of Memory in Medieval Culture* (Cambridge: Cambridge University Press, 1991).

2. Walter Benjamin, "Über den Begriff der Geschichte," in Walter Benjamin, *Gesammelten Schriften*, vol. 1, part 2 (Frankfurt: Suhrkamp, 1974), 693-704, here

With this claim and with the other theses, Benjamin opposed a way of remembering the past and writing history that presupposed time to be a homogenous, empty continuum indifferently filled up with this or that chain of events. On his view, this is a central presupposition of "historicism." For historicism, he argued, the task of history is simply to depict that chain of events, "the way it really happened." The historian is to trace different causal links, gradually identifying those links that make up the chain leading to our own present. The past is conceded no other claim on the present, no presence, not even the presence of absence: the mournful absence of a past era's future, chains in which the links were shattered and the chain thus interrupted by natural or historical catastrophe. Or, to be more precise, the only past that historicism allows to be present is the one that survived: it is the future that derives from the victors' past that dominates such a history. The hopes and dreams of those who were vanquished are forgotten; they have no further claim or influence on our present.

Benjamin insists, in contrast, that the historian's task is "to brush history against the grain," by letting those forgotten hopes from the past reemerge in the present.[3] Remembering the past and recounting its history must mean "fanning into flame those sparks of hope that are found in the past."[4] Benjamin does not shy from theological language: this is to redeem the past. For the person who brushes history against the grain "the past has a secret index, by which it is referred to redemption."[5] The historian "grasps the constellation in which his own era comes into contact with a quite specific earlier one. Thus he establishes a conception of the present as the 'time of the now' [*Jetztzeit*] which is shot through with shards of Messianic time."[6] It is the capacity to do this, to allow a repressed or vanished hope from the past to flare up anew to inspire the present, that Benjamin names a "*weak* messianic power."[7]

---

704. For the English translation of the theses, see *Illuminations*, ed. Hannah Arendt; trans. Harry Zohn (New York: Schocken, 1968), 253-64, here 264.

3. Benjamin, "Über den Begriff der Geschichte," 697.

4. Ibid., 695.

5. Ibid., 693.

6. Ibid. 704.

7. Ibid., 694. Emphasis in original.

Metz draws heavily on Benjamin in formulating his category of "dangerous memory," although the influence of Herbert Marcuse is also palpable.[8] We remember the suffering of past generations, but also their joys, hopes, aspirations, and dreams, many of which were cut short, left unfulfilled by unjustly inflicted suffering and death. Taking this stance toward the past entails taking a stance toward the future such that these hopes have a share in the future envisioned from our hopes. It is the only stance that opens up a truly human, humane future. It is also, Metz worries (thinking particularly of European forgetfulness of the Holocaust), a stance that is being increasingly repressed in Europe, too often with the tacit complicity of the church. For Metz—not incidentally for our theme as we shall see when we take up Gutiérrez's reflections on memory—the degree to which the church is so complicit marks also the degree to which it represses and denies its constitutive roots in Judaism. In the 1980s, and even more so after the reunification of Germany, Nietzsche became the primary interlocutor in Metz's unveiling of this danger of individual and cultural amnesia: "Nietzsche came up with the motto, 'Blessed are the forgetful,' intentionally echoing the biblical beatitude, 'Blessed are those who mourn.'"[9] Modern scientific-technological society is, on Metz's reading, making this motto its own.

Under the quasi-mythical totality of technical rationality what threatens us is an intelligence without pathos, an intelligence that has no need for any insistent and obstinate speech because it functions smoothly, without any contradictions or conflicts, an intelligence that knows nothing of memory, precisely because it is not threatened by forgetting: the person as computerized intelligence, without any sensitivity to suffering and without any morality: in short, a rhapsody of innocence congealed into a smoothly functioning machine.[10]

---

8. Johann Baptist Metz cites him, along with Benjamin, in *Faith in History and Society*, rev. trans. (New York: Crossroad, 2004), 177-78. His principal source is Herbert Marcuse, *Eros and Civilization: A Philosophical Inquiry into Freud* (New York: Vintage Books, 1955).

9. Johann Baptist Metz, *Memoria passionis: Ein provozierendes Gedächtnis in pluralistischer Gesellschaft* (Freiburg im Breisgau: Herder, 2006), 139.

10. Metz, *Memoria passionis*, 80.

Against this backdrop Metz argues that the essential gift that Judaism and Christianity offer to modernity is an understanding of reason for which memory, in the sense that Benjamin outlined it, is indispensable, is constitutive. As an antidote to the scientifically, technologically oriented rationality of the Enlightenment—"instrumental reason," as Adorno and Horkheimer named it—and in contrast to Jürgen Habermas's counterproposal of a "communicative reason," Metz asserts the need to recover, recognize, and nourish *anamnestic* reason.

One entry point into understanding what he means by anamnestic reason is to tarry a while with his intriguing discussion of technical rationality, of a computerized intelligence "which knows nothing of forgetting, and hence, of course, of remembering either."[11] Despite its increasingly comprehensive and unassailable mastery of data from the past, the computer does not remember; and neither does human reason that takes its measure by the cybernetic power of recall. What might he mean by this?

Here again, Benjamin's influence is decisive. To disclose this influence we return to his use of the theme of redemption and "weak messianic power." "Of course," Benjamin writes, "only a redeemed humanity can fully inherit its past—which is to say that only for redeemed humanity can its past become citable in all its moments."[12] Only from the perspective of a total redemption do *all* the possible futures of all past moments find appropriate fulfillment. In the face of such a daunting, indeed impossible, task, we have, Benjamin insists, only a *weak* messianic power. We can draw only a few of those shattered or repressed moments of the past into the light of the present and allow them to live again, however fleetingly, in our own hopes and aspirations—there can be only *shards* of messianic time in our present. Thus, all our remembering is surrounded by a penumbra of

---

11. *Faith in History and Society*, 181.

12. Benjamin, "Über den Begriff der Geschichte," 694. Theodor Adorno wrote in a similar vein, that philosophy is "the effort to regard all things the way they would represent themselves from the standpoint of redemption. Knowledge has no other light than that which shines from redemption on the world; all others exhaust themselves in *post facto* construction and remain a part of technology" (*Minima Moralia: Reflexionen aus dem beschädigten Leben* [Frankfurt: Surhkamp, 1951], 480).

forgetting; our remembering is threatened by forgetting, and consequently our knowing too, to the extent that, as humans, our knowing
is always inflected by the kind of future that, in hope, in despair, or
in melancholic indifference, we project for the present we know now.
To recognize this constitutive and ineluctable threatenedness of our
remembering—which is not to overcome it—is to allow an element of
mourning to find its way into all our remembering and our knowing.
This is the price of envisioning, and hoping in, a future that is more
than a continuation of the history of the victors.

The computerized intelligence fills the empty, homogenous continuum of time with chains of events, without reference to that in them
which is unfulfilled and unredeemed. It does not really remember.
While the lack of certain data from the past can render some of its
chains of events more or less probable, this intelligence is not really
"threatened" by forgetting, as is human memory and the anamnestic
reason connected with it. But neither can it hope for any future other
than the extrapolation or "evolution" of the present.[13] A remembering
in which the past—including the past that *cannot* be fully recalled—
becomes genuinely, often disturbingly present, even if only in a
mournful sense, for what is absent is impossible to it.

Human beings can and do forget; by the same token, human beings
genuinely remember. This constitutes both the threat to memory and
its proper dignity. Human memory is finite; like human knowing in
general it is inescapably selective: some past moments, but not others,
are present in a particular way, modulated by particular hopes that
informed those past moments, while others recede into the penum-
bral background of forgetting. Some are simply lost without possible
recall, because all their traces were annihilated. How can these forgotten elements of the past still be authentically present to us, shaping
our understanding of the present and our hopes and planning for the
future? Metz answers that this is possible only by virtue of a particular
sense for the past, a mood in the present that springs from our awareness of the fragility of memory, of its constitutive being-threatened-by
forgetting. This knowledge of and sense for what has been lost, for
what is missing, *Vermissenswissen,* as Metz names it, becomes for him

---

13. Hence Metz's worry about "a new quasi metaphysics. Its name: the logic of
evolution" (*Faith in History and Society*, 158).

a genuinely mystical disposition by virtue of which that which has been forgotten from the past, residing in the penumbra surrounding what we remember at any given moment, is always ready to be "redeemed," flaring up like an ember in the present.[14] It is our dignity and charge as free human subjects to be open to the claim that these memories might make upon us, and to resist any historicism that would relegate them to the utter darkness of permanent forgetfulness. This is all the more the case when it is not just the ineluctable finitude of the human condition that links forgetting and remembering, but human sinfulness and pride, or the repression of the guilt that accompanies the insight that our history is marked by sin, and that the blood of those who were killed along the way cries out from the ground.[15] Metz names this complex way that human beings relate to the past, and through that to their present and future, the "dialectic of remembering and forgetting."[16]

Thus far with Benjamin. Yet for Metz, unlike Benjamin, our own reliance on a "weak" messianic power can only be conceived as being carried by the "strong" messianic power of the God of Jesus: "the God of the living and of the dead, the God who touches even past suffering, who does not leave even the dead in their repose."[17] We can only bear the finitude and sinful guilt of our "anamnestic reason" as we turn, in prayer, to the saving God for whom full redemption is possible—indeed, has been brought to pass. And this turning too is rooted in memory: the memory of the passion, death, and resurrection of Jesus. Christian hope draws on the remembrance of Jesus' suffering and death, but also the memory of his resurrection as the redemption of that past life and the pledge of fulfillment for the hope that oriented it: the full coming of God's kingdom and the comprehensive redemp-

---

14. Benjamin, "Über den Begriff der Geschichte," 695.

15. As Benjamin puts it, "There has never been a document of culture which has not at the same time been a document of barbarism" ("Über den Begriff der Geschichte," 696).

16. On the dialectic of remembering and forgetting, and its relation to anamnestic reason as a "Vermissenswissen," see Metz, *Memoria passionis*, xi, 3-11, 28f., 123, 222-25, 256.

17. Johann Baptist Metz, *A Passion for God: The Mystical-Political Dimension of Christianity,* ed. and trans. with intro. by J. Matthew Ashley (Mahwah, NJ: Paulist Press, 1998), 188 n. 27.

tion it symbolizes. But while he introduces God as the salvific frame for the dialectic of human remembering and forgetting, Metz does not investigate further whether the human dialectic of remembering and forgetting might even characterize God. For this we turn to Gustavo Gutiérrez and his reflections on a *Dios memorioso.*

Gustavo Gutiérrez and God's Memory
of the Least Ones

Gustavo Gutiérrez frequently uses a saying of the great Dominican advocate of the Indians, Bartolomé de Las Casas, to enter into a discussion of God's memory: *Del más chiquito y del más olvidado, Dios tiene la memoria muy viva y muy reciente* ("Of the littlest and most forgotten, God has a very fresh and vivid memory").[18] Gutiérrez insists that "the God of the Bible is a God richly endowed with memory, a God who does not forget the covenant that God establishes with God's people."[19] As I shall attempt to show, his reflections on God's memory provides a perfect counterpart to Metz's proposal of an anamnestic reason characterized by *Vermissenswissen.*

As does Metz, Gutiérrez distinguishes memory from a cybernetic compilation of past events:

Memory is not history, if by the latter we understand a simple relating of past events. . . . Memory is the present of the past that has its source in the ever present and indefectible love of God. This is a crucial insight, which makes of history a theophany, a revelation of God that calls to life and rejects every form of unjust death.[20]

Remembering makes of God's saving acts in history an urgent challenge *now* to act in accord with them, as Gutiérrez notes, citing Deuteronomy 5:3: "Not with our ancestors did the LORD make this covenant, but with us, who are all of us here alive today," and the Gospel of

---

18. Quoted in "Memoria y profecía," in *Gustavo Gutiérrez, textos esenciales: acordarse de los pobres*, ed Andrés Gallego (Lima: Fondo Editorial del Congreso del Perú, 2004), 255-78, here 257. Henceforth cited as MP. English translations are my own.

19. MP, 259.

20. MP, 258f.

Luke: "Today this scripture has been fulfilled in your hearing" (4:21).
The Bible (and the Hebrew Bible in particular) speaks of memory not
only in the context of the people's memory but as a crucial mediation
on God's side of the relationship between God and God's people. God
remembers God's covenant with the people to the thousandth generation. Indeed, in virtue of God's remembering, God can be called on
to *forget* the people's sins as an expression of the freely given love that
is the foundation of the covenant, and the indestructible fidelity by
means of which that love stretches itself out through time (see, among
other passages, Psalms 25:7; 79:8; 106:40-46). Gutiérrez hints in this
way at a dialectic of remembering and forgetting that structures God's
presence in and to history. This suggests intercalating Metz's elaboration of that dialectic into the theology of God that Gutiérrez lays out.

If, as Metz suggests, it is true that "forgetting" is an element of
remembering (and not just as a threat to memory, but rather as integral to its dignity), and if we can, with necessary caveats about analogical predication, think about God in these terms, then I suggest
the following continuation of Gutiérrez's observations. If there be a
"selectivity" to God's memory, a forgetting, it is a selectivity governed
by God's free and sovereign love—God's love for the people God has
chosen as God's own, and God's love, in particular, for the least ones.[21]
The ones to whom society concedes no future ("forgets") are the ones
for whom God has "a fresh and living memory." They, and they in
particular, have a future.[22] In God's preferential remembering—governed by the love that is given concrete shape in the covenant—God
also "forgets" the sins of God's people. These sins, and the ways of life
to which they give shape, are accorded no future. They recede into
the fringes of forgetfulness. From this perspective the preferential-
ity of God's love manifests itself in the way that God remembers and
forgets: turning God's back on sin and its concretizations in history so
that they have no future; remembering those whom everyone else has
forgotten so that they do have a future.

---

21. As Gutiérrez notes, this selectivity can even extend beyond the limits of
God's chosen people, as Jonah's experience in Ninevah demonstrated (to Jonah's
distress): MP 259.

22. One thinks here of the words the prophet Jeremiah was instructed by God
to convey to the exiles in Babylon: "I know the plans I have for you . . . plans for
your welfare and not for harm, to give you a future with hope" (Jeremiah 29:11).

This remembering on God's part presses a claim in turn on how the people of God are to remember. In the Hebrew Bible the people are called to make God's memory their own, which means making their own God's remembering of those who are overlooked and marginalized: the widow, the orphan, the stranger. This requires a different way of understanding the present and extrapolating the future. Gutiérrez reminds us that "The giving of the law and of norms of conduct begins with 'Remember that you were a slave in the land of Egypt, and the LORD your God brought you out from there . . .' and similar phrases (Deuteronomy 5:15; 15:15; 16:12)."[23] The New Testament also emphasizes remembering God's past action as the key for the community's present action:

> The gratuitous love of God, the heart of biblical revelation, is the model for the believer's action; it is the most important thing we remember, acting like a "north star" that orients the community of followers of Jesus, whose task it is to be precisely a sign of this love in history."[24]

Discerning this "north star" is tantamount to "reading the signs of the times." On the one hand, it allows us to perceive new possibilities. The strength and constancy of God's memory open us to the novelty of God's will for the future—every moment becomes indeed a "strait gate through which the Messiah might enter." For Gutiérrez, this is particularly important in a postmodern age that often creates "a certain skepticism whose consequences run the gamut from passivity to despair when it comes to possibilities for changing the status quo."[25] We have already seen in Metz's thought the power of memory for breaking the power of "the status quo." Gutiérrez notes that the community unleashes this power by giving flesh to the memory of God in its own vision and action, enfleshing in particular God's memory of the least ones and the forgotten:

> Called to live out the impact of God's memory in our time, this will allow us to see that new and promising clues for living together socially are woven into it, both for the life of faith and

---

23. Ibid., 260.
24. Ibid.
25. Ibid., 275.

for finding pathways that open us in a vital and creative way to the gift of hope. Theology, to the extent that it is an interpretation of hope, a hermeneutic of hope, has an important role to play in this.[26]

Finally, to the extent that we succeed in doing this, we incarnate anew God's memory, which is to say that we give testimony to it. Gutiérrez expresses this complex interweaving of God's memory, the memory of the people, their action in history, and the role of theology, in the following summary statement of the significance of Bartolomé de Las Casas:

> Las Casas always had the sense that the situation of the Indies represented something tremendously novel. Coming to terms with it required categories that were equally novel. One of them, and the most important for him, is reading and rereading events "as if we were Indians," from the perspective of the poor in whom Christ is present. This is not only a question of theological methodology, but has to do with the journey toward the God of life. It was the way of making his own the fresh and living memory that God has for the smallest and the most forgotten. Testimonies like those of Monsignor Angelelli, Mons. Romero and so many others in Latin America, make this memory present among us.[27]

Las Casas's theological genius consisted in his ability to find the tools to elaborate theologically a key spiritual insight, which Gutiérrez describes as that of "seeing in the Indian, in this Other of the Western world, the poor that the gospel tells us about. . . . This evangelical and mystical intuition [Gutiérrez continues] is the root of his spirituality."[28] I suggest that we think of this as a mystical union that has its center in the human capacity for memory, properly understood. This mystical union transforms human memory, and thus human subjectivity. It gave Las Casas a powerful presence and orientating wisdom in the

---

26. Ibid.

27. Gustavo Gutiérrez, "Memoria de Dios y anuncio del evangelio (el testimonio de Bartolomé de Las Casas)," in *Gustavo Gutiérrez, textos esenciales*, 495-513, here 513.

28. Ibid.

turbulent world of "old" and "new" Spain. Las Casas became in this way a witness to the memory of God; and to the extent that his testimony was successful (always in the power of the Holy Spirit), that memory becomes available in a new, enspiriting way for the church as a whole.

Conclusion: Theology as Hermeneutic of Hope; Mysticism as a Union of Memories

It may well be that the urgency of remembering correctly in this age of atrocities is part of the impetus behind the currency of the topic of memory.[29] Indeed, some, like Miroslav Volf, have argued that some memories need to be forgotten—an assertion that can both be affirmed and denied on the basis just laid. Much more can and must be done to explore a theology that is a *memoria quaerens intellectum*. I make here two concluding remarks to flesh out my suggestion that the praxis of memory/testimony evident in the Latin American martyrs can be understood in terms of a mystical union in which the locus of union with God is found not so much in intellect or will—the two options explored in the Middle Ages—as in memory.

First, I have suggested that we speak of a union of memories in which our memory, defined by the dialectic of remembering and forgetting, is united with and conformed to the memory of God, who remembers even and especially those consigned by a sinful history to an oblivion that resists even the most resolute attempts to remember them by human means. Is this not the condition for the possibility of the redemption of which Walter Benjamin wrote, without, perhaps, really believing it possible? Such a mysticism would have a dark night of its own, since it would bring not so much the capacity to remember all past events (any more than medievals understood the mystical union of beatific vision, located in human reason, to confer omniscience, or to render the mystery of God understandable for the

---

29. See Miroslav Volf, *The End of Memory: Remembering Rightly in a Violent World* (Grand Rapids: Eerdmans, 2006). The work of John de Gruchy and Robert Schreiter on the necessity and necessary conditions for reconciliation in the aftermath of violent conflict is also significant in this context. I first learned of these texts because of the work of two of my students in particular, Ernesto Valiente and Candace McLean, whose own dissertation projects on the theology of reconciliation and on memory (respectively) have led me to many insights.

still-finite human intellect). Rather it requires and nourishes an intensification of that sense of what is absent in our remembering: Metz's
Vermissenswissen, a presence to the past suspended on the border
of remembering and forgetting, in which we not only mourn more
deeply, but celebrate and hope more radically—and, finally, act more
faithfully in history, "walking humbly before God in history," to borrow a line from Jon Sobrino.[30]

Second, located in that human capacity that ties us ineluctably to
history, such a mysticism, or such a way of articulating mysticism,
promises to pay dividends for understanding better that genus in the
history of Christian spirituality known as "contemplation in action."
In fact, the perspective offered here opens a path to an argument that
the emergence of this category of contemplation *in* action at the end
of the Middle Ages should be looked upon as the emergence of a tacit
exploration of precisely the kind of mysticism of union of memories
that is otherwise the "road less taken" by the great medieval mystics.
To take the species in this genus represented by the martyrs of the
Universidad Centroamericana, I suggest further that an underappre-
ciated aspect of Ignatian spirituality, and of the *Spiritual Exercises* in
particular, is the way it opens the way to a transformation of memory. In the exercises of the so-called Second and Third Weeks of the
Spiritual Exercises, one is to remember—in a vivid and self-involving
way—the events of Jesus' life, work, suffering, death, and resurrection,
with the goal of making of our lives a testimony to that memory. Only
in this kind of remembering can the "election" be made: the life-deter-
mining decision regarding how one's life can more fully "praise, reverence, and serve God." In the well-known concluding exercise, "The
Contemplation to Attain Love for God," the one making the retreat
is constantly urged to remember all the good that God has done for
her or him. In the culminating prayer of this exercise in remembering, the *Suscipe,* he or she offers to God "all my liberty, my *memory,*
my understanding, my entire will and all I have and possess."[31] If the

---

30. See Jon Sobrino, "Spirituality and the Following of Jesus," in *Mysterium
Liberationis: Fundamental Concepts of Liberation Theology,* ed. Jon Sobrino and
Ignacio Ellacuría (Maryknoll, NY: Orbis Books, 1993), 697; Jon Sobrino, *Christ
the Liberator: A View from the Victims* (Maryknoll, NY: Orbis Books, 2001), 338-
40.

31. Ignatius of Loyola, *Spiritual Exercises,* no. 234. Emphasis added.

offer of freedom marks the desire for unconditional openness to the will of God—the spiritual disposition of indifference—the offer of memory marks, I suggest, an opening to a transformation of memory that gives concrete substance to the offer of one's will and provides its orienting "north star": which is to unite our memory with God's "fresh and vivid memory of the littlest and most forgotten."

12

New Eyes and a New Home: Oscar Romero's Conversion as a Response to Social Sin

Michael E. Lee

When reflecting on the *testimonio* of Archbishop Oscar Romero, and particularly how to receive that testimony here in the United States, the central question is, "Do we have eyes to see and ears to hear?" There is a twofold danger. First, there is the danger that we don't want to hear Romero's testimony. For example, there is the 2010 decision of the Texas school board to remove any mention of Romero from its high school textbooks.[1] For others, the witness of an archbishop of the Roman Catholic Church carries with it too much baggage from that institution's failings. Still others will find other obstacles that allow them to reject Romero as irrelevant or too great a challenge to their interests or ways of thinking.

However, more insidious perhaps is the danger for those who would accept Romero's testimony at some level, those that, though they are willing to receive his testimony, are unable—either through a distanciation (a focusing on the spectacular, which diminishes Romero's capacity to challenge) or a proximization (a domesticating of Romero that waters down his challenge to vague moral epithets). More than geographic distance, more than chronological distance, more than hermeneutic distance, those in the economically prosper-

---

1. A decision Jon Stewart wryly described as "how Oscar Romero got disappeared by right-wingers for the second time," in "Don't Mess with Textbooks," *The Daily Show*, March 17, 2010 (http://www.thedailyshow.com/watch/wed-march-17-2010/don-t-mess-with-textbooks).

ous North are confronted with a distance of historical reality to hear Romero's testimony, and this demands a journey for which the church has only begun to develop a language.

For all that has been written on social sin and the preferential option for the poor, there are ways to rationalize and co-opt. We may begrudgingly admit the existence of social ills in our country, but as a church, we struggle to name white privilege and sexism. A Catholic vice-presidential candidate proposed a draconian budget and called it a preferential option for the poor. Clearly, no amount of words, no amount of rational arguments will suffice. What is needed is conversion, and if conversion is needed, then I would maintain that Romero himself provides us a way to understand and undergo that conversion.

In this essay, I would like to consider a fuller understanding of conversion revealed in Romero's testimony in three claims: (1) that the transformation Romero experienced as he became archbishop should be called a conversion, but one conceived not as a response to a singular dramatic event but an evolution prompted by confronting the reality of poverty; (2) that at the heart of Romero's conversion is a new way of seeing, and that seeing is the "realization" of social sin and its historical demands; and (3) that Romero's conversion culminates in and embodies a preferential option for the poor, a response that simultaneously may be described as a wrestling with the uncanny legacy of colonial injustice.

Obviously, to speak of a person's conversion cannot mean fully capturing that complex dynamic that is ultimately the human encounter with the mystery of God. Only hubris could claim to possess "the" story of Romero's conversion. To speak of Romero's conversion in the United States is not to speak from a position of power that gets to dictate the terms and manipulate the results. It is to speak from a place of need, a place of lack: the place that fears that, like the young man from the gospel story, after standing before Jesus and justifying ourselves, we might ultimately turn away, unable to respond to the invitation: "There is one more thing you need. Give all that you have to the poor, and come follow me." With this in mind, let me turn to that remarkable transformation of Oscar Romero and how it can help us think anew about conversion.

Oscar Romero's Evolutionary Conversion

Many who know little else about Romero can recite this basic narrative. Oscar Romero is named archbishop of San Salvador in February of 1977. While powerful elements of the Salvadoran church and society view this appointment with satisfaction, other priests, catechists, and base communities are bitterly disappointed. However, something momentous occurs to Romero that transforms him from the conservative cleric he had been into a bold prophet and champion of the poor. On March 12, 1977, just three weeks after Romero's installation as archbishop, the Jesuit priest Rutilio Grande is assassinated along with the seventy-two-year-old Manuel Solorzando and sixteen-year-old Nelson Rutilio Lemus.[2] Romero, confronted by the brutality of his close friend's murder, undergoes an inconceivable change that sets the course of his ministry as archbishop in a completely different direction. As Robert McDermott puts it, "For the new archbishop, the murder [of Rutilio Grande] was a moment of truth. As he prayed over his dead friend, he was faced with conversion—a New Testament-style *metanoia*. He knew that he would have to choose sides."[3]

As a narrative, this account of Romero's conversion is compelling. It possesses a dramatic arc and articulates some important reasons why there is and should be deep respect for this remarkable figure.[4] Yet, it is the very drama of the story, the sudden nature of the narration, that can distort the testimony and make of conversion something not only dramatic but implicitly remote from the experience of the average Christian.

While the change that took place in Romero's life as he became archbishop of San Salvador is often described as a conversion, the

---

2. It is telling how often the names of those accompanying Grande, the seventy-two-year-old Manuel Solorzano and Nelson Rutilio Lemus, sixteen, are not mentioned.

3. Robert T. McDermott, "In the Footsteps of Martyrs: Lessons from Central America," in *Romero's Legacy: The Call to Peace and Justice*, ed. Pilar Hogan Closkey and John P. Hogan (Lanham, MD: Rowman & Littlefield, 2007), 19. Similarly, Ken Woodward writes, "It was the incident that, by his own account, emboldened Romero to accept a larger, prophetic role as the voice of the Salvadoran people" (Woodward, *Making Saints* [New York: Simon & Schuster, 1990], 41).

4. The ubiquity of this narrative also testifies to the influence of the Paulist film *Romero* throughout the U.S. Catholic community.

appropriateness and meaning of this description are not always clear. For example, consider William James's classic definition of conversion as occurring when "religious ideas, previously peripheral in [a person's] consciousness, now take a central place, and religious aims form the habitual center of [her/his] energy."[5] Romero's experience after becoming archbishop does not involve moving from unbelief to belief. Throughout the course of Romero's life, one in which he was born into a Catholic family and aspired to priesthood even as a boy, we see religious aims at the center of Romero's energy.

Similarly, Romero's change cannot be classified as a sudden repentance from personal sin. From his childhood through his decades as a priest, Romero recognized all too well his own sinfulness and the need for forgiveness. Indeed, if anything, Romero's spirituality over his lifetime was marked more by an inclination to scrupulosity regarding his sinfulness than the need for a fundamental reorientation and conversion.

This is not meant to deny a dramatic element to Romero's experience. With Walter Conn we can affirm that a born Christian may experience a "cognitive, affective, moral, and faith transformation which a new and vital relationship with the person of Christ effects."[6] However, we need not see this transformation as divorced or as a significant departure from the rest of a person's life. For Karl Rahner, conversion is experienced as "the gift of God's grace . . . and as radical, fundamental decision which concerns *a human life in its entirety*, even when it is realized in a particular concrete decision in everyday life."[7] Related intimately with that "fundamental option," we can affirm Oscar Romero's change in relation to the whole of his life. Conversion is not a violent, divine intervention, but the dynamic coincidence of God's grace and human response in freedom. This

---

5. William James, *Varieties of Religious Experience* Lecture IX (Oxford: Oxford University Press, 2012), 98. James also uses the notion of unity so that conversion is "the process, gradual or sudden, by which a self hitherto divided, and consciously wrong and unhappy, becomes unified and consciously right, superior and happy, in consequence of its firmer hold upon religious realities."

6. Walter Conn, *Christian Conversion: A Developmental Interpretation of Autonomy and Surrender* (Mahwah, NJ: Paulist Press, 1986), 198.

7. Karl Rahner, "Conversion," in *Encyclopedia of Theology: A Concise Sacramentum Mundi* (London: Burn & Oates, 1975), 291 (emphasis added).

coincidence, though it might be marked by certain moments of intensification, must be placed within a complex network of interactions that are biographical, psychological, historical, social, etc., and span across a lifetime.

This is why most commentators on Romero prefer, as indeed Romero himself did, to speak of his transformation in terms of a process, an evolution. Though this evolution might be seen as culminating or at least intensified in the Grande assassination, it is one that stretches over a longer period of time. In June 1978, Romero addressed the question of his conversion in a visit to Cardinal Baggio, prefect of the Congregation of Bishops. Baggio expressed his displeasure with the idea that Romero had been converted and that Romero might see himself as a prophet as opposed to his fellow bishops who had not been "converted."[8] Romero responded to these allegations vehemently,

> I denied having used the phrase attributed to me of "having been converted" and much less having compared myself to the other bishops or vainly believing myself "a prophet." What happened in my priestly life, I have tried to explain to myself as an evolution of the same desire that I have always had to be faithful to what God asks of me.[9]

Many of Romero's closest associates affirm that he rejected a dramatic notion of conversion in his self-understanding. Ricardo Urioste, Romero's vicar general says, "I believe that Monseñor Romero was someone who always, throughout his life, sought conversion," but qualifies this by adding that "[Romero] never spoke of himself in terms of conversion; he spoke of evolution."[10] Similarly, Bishop Gregorio Rosa Chávez relates that he asked Romero directly if

---

8. Translations of portions of the Romero–Baggio correspondence can be found in the Brockman–Romero Papers, DePaul University Archives (DPUA).

9. These words come from a memo that Romero wrote to Baggio three days after their meeting as a summary and reflection on their conversation, DPUA, Brockman–Romero Collection, Box 2.

10. Ricardo Urioste Bustamante, "Monseñor Romero: Martyr for the Magisterium," in Robert Pelton CSC, ed., *Archbishop Romero: Martyr and Prophet for the New Millennium* (Scranton, PA: University of Scranton Press, 2006), 47-57, at 55.

he had been converted, to which Romero responded, "I wouldn't say it's been a conversion, but an evolution."[11]

The importance of speaking about Romero's transformation as an evolution is that it does justice to the entirety of Romero's life—his childhood and familial influences, his thirty-five years of ordained ministry, and the personal faith that Romero possessed and nurtured prior to the dramatic events of 1977. It provides a more complex and integrative concept of change than an instantaneous transformation.

More proximately, understanding Romero's conversion as an evolution places it, and the Grande assassination, in a wider context that acknowledges the importance of that period between 1974 and 1977 when Romero served as bishop in Santiago de María, the diocese that included his hometown of Ciudad Barrios. As Zacarías Díez and Juan Macho relate, it was there that Romero confronted the misery and oppression of *campesinos*, the many small children dying of preventable diseases and malnutrition, and the repressive violence against those who would raise a voice in protest for justice.[12] Travelling to small villages on horseback and opening the doors of the diocesan house during cold winter nights of the coffee harvest, Romero confronted a reality that he had forgotten, repressed, or at least allowed to fade to the periphery of his concerns. Whatever the case, when speaking of Romero's change, the time in Santiago de María must be counted as a crucial period in his evolution and offers a glimpse into the content of Romero's conversion.

Thus, the language of evolution helpfully draws attention to the continuity of Romero's life-long journey of faith and more richly accounts for the complex process through which the events of 1977 can be seen as a culmination. Any change in Romero at that time should be seen within the longer journey of Romero's faith, and furthermore, as a moment in a transformation that continued over the course of Romero's time as archbishop. As Romero himself would attest, conversion is continual.

Locking Romero's conversion into the months of February and

---

11. Gregorio Rosa Chávez, "Archbishop Romero: A Bishop for the New Millennium," in ibid., 33-45, at 34.

12. Zacarías Díez and Juan Macho, *En Santiago de María me tope con la miseria* (San Salvador: Imprenta Criterio, 1995).

March of 1977 ultimately presents an ahistorical view of conversion and ignores the process he would continue until his assassination in March of 1980. Moreover, in a context outside of that moment in Salvadoran history, the focus on the dramatic can displace Romero's challenge. If we can chalk Romero's conversion up to the spectacular, then we can keep it distant from our ordinary lives. On a pedestal, Romero cannot speak to us directly. We enact the worry that Dorothy Day voiced when asked about her own possible canonization, "Don't call me a saint. I don't want to be dismissed so easily."

Oscaro Romero's Conversion as Seeing Anew

Though seeing Romero's conversion as an evolution avoids the distortion of distancing, its emphasis on continuity should not obscure the sense of real and radical change that took place in Romero's life in 1977. To be sure, there was a real change in Romero after he became archbishop that should not be overlooked or glossed over. As Romero's successor, Bishop Arturo Rivera Damas, states,

> I agree with those who speak of a "conversion" of Monseñor Romero, in the moment in which he assumed the pastoral charge of the archdiocese of San Salvador. . . . Before the body of Fr. Rutilio Grande, Monseñor Romero, on his twentieth day as archbishop, felt the call of Christ to defeat his natural human timidity and to fill himself with the intrepidness of the apostle.[13]

This intrepidness in Romero's preaching and actions marked a significant change in Romero's life and ministry, and it is in exploring that change that we can specify the content of Romero's conversion and how his legacy continues to challenge.

With more space, I could explore specific moments in which Romero evidences a change in temperament and action. Among them: his calling for Grande's funeral Mass to be the only Mass in the country (the *misa única*); his personal boycott of General Humberto Romero's presidential inauguration—bold public defiance where once he worked only behind the scenes; his support of the Colegio

---

13. Preface to Jesus Delgado, *Oscar A. Romero: Biografía* (San Salvador: UCA, 1990), 3. It is cited and translated in Douglas Marcouiller, "Archbishop with an Attitude: Oscar Romero's *Sentir con la Iglesia*," *Studies in the Spirituality of Jesuits* 35.3 (May 2003): 19.

El Sagrado Corazón in marked contrast to his actions in the so-called Externado affair; the openness theologically to ideas and figures such as Jon Sobrino, whom he once found suspicious; his seeking advice and collaboration where he once was aloof and private. These all speak to a real change in Romero; and if we are to call that change a conversion, they raise the question about the content of that conversion. From what did Romero "turn"?

In some sense, the resistance and criticism that Romero faced make clear that his *conversio* was a turning away from something. Maria López Vigil's biography of Romero recounts the reaction of wealthy San Salvadorans who had their gifts of a house and car rejected by Romero: "They say that when the hoity-toity women of San Salvador realized how Monseñor Romero was changing, they got offended and said, 'That boy has turned out to have very bad manners!'"[14] Romero's own diary entry of August 21, 1979, notes an encounter with a woman from one of the Salvadoran wealthy families who said Romero is "not the same as before and that I deceived them." He reflects, "I understand that this calumny is common in those who do not want the Church to touch their petty interests."[15]

Of course this turning-away-from also meant a turning toward something else. For Carmen Alvarez, it was that Romero had formerly lived away from reality (*¡por los aguacates!*) but now saw the reality of the poor. Other commentators also use the metaphor of sight, which can signal not just the radical shift from blindness (seeing nothing) to sight (seeing), but also a deepening of sight (a seeing more fully). Ricardo Urioste likens Romero's conversion to the healing of the blind man from Bethsaida in the Gospel of Mark (Mark 8:22-26). As Jesus heals the man by putting spittle in his eyes, he sees blurry figures at first. Only upon being touched by Jesus again does he see with clarity. It is not that Romero had no compassion for the poor before becoming archbishop, nor that he did not take great measures to care for the poor. However, his conversion marks a new seeing, a new clarity about the reality in which he lived.

Jon Sobrino also uses a visual metaphor when stating that as "Arch-

---

14. María López Vigil, *Memories in Mosaic,* trans. Kathy Ogle (Washington, DC: EPICA, 2000; Maryknoll, NY: Orbis Books, 2013), 121.

15. Oscar Romero, *A Shepherd's Diary,* trans. Irene B. Hodgson (Cincinnati: St. Anthony Messenger, 1993), 311.

bishop Romero stood gazing at the mortal remains of Rutilio Grande, the scales fell from his eyes."[16] He invokes the dramatic Pauline conversion to stress that what Romero saw was that Grande died as Jesus died. Grande's ministry, which took flesh among the poor of Aguilares, was one that more clearly reflected the following of Jesus and would then redirect Romero's ministry as archbishop.

As we have seen, in a certain respect, it is important to distinguish the "new sight" of Romero's conversion from the turning away from sin. Martin Maier, in his study of Romero's spirituality, concludes that Romero's conversion is best understood not as a turning from sin, but, drawing from the Rules for Discernment in the *Spiritual Exercises* of St. Ignatius of Loyola, as a movement *de lo bueno a lo mejor,* "from the good to the better."[17] This movement is characterized by a "seeing anew," a radical change in understanding and putting into action the will of God. Romero's own assessment, when asked about his conversion during the CELAM meeting at Puebla in early 1978, seems to support Maier's claim.

> To be converted is to turn to the true God, and in that sense I feel that my contact with the poor, with the needy, leads to a growing sense of need for God. . . . In this sense, then, I too seek conversion, in order to be able to put my trust in God and through God be able to provide a word of consolation, a response to the poor's anguish, and if possible point out the way to those who can resolve these predicaments.[18]

The seeing anew that Romero experiences is a turning to God prompted by his encounter with the reality of poverty, whether in Santiago de María or in the murders of Fr. Grande, Don Manuel, and young Tilo. However, I would argue that, in our globalized context, we not move too quickly away from the notion of a turning from sin, and that we understand Romero's "seeing," his growing sense of the need for God, in relation to a profound realization of social sin.

---

16. Jon Sobrino, *Archbishop Romero: Memories and Reflections,* trans. Robert R. Barr (Maryknoll, NY: Orbis Books, 1990), 17.

17. Martin Meier, *Monseñor Romero, maestro de espiritualidad* (San Salvador: UCA Editores, 2005), 104.

18. As cited in James R. Brockman, *Romero: A Life* (Maryknoll, NY: Orbis Books, 2005), 160.

Romero's conversion signals a link between the realization of social sin and an incarnation to confront that sin. To understand it this way, one must shift the consideration of social sin from a juridical to a historical framework. This does not mean ignoring a sense of causal responsibility for social ills. Romero's realization of social sin in El Salvador and the corresponding form of repentance and action would be qualitatively different from that of the landed oligarch who refused to pay fair wages, or the paramilitary who carried out acts of repression. Yet, Romero's response forces us to reckon with what Kenneth Himes calls "distributive moral responsibility," where liability for social sin can merit a response from a person even if there is not a direct responsibility (as causal) or culpability (as evaluative, blameworthiness).[19] The key we find in Romero is how that response takes historical flesh. Romero put it plainly in a homily of December 1979, by noting, "A rich person finds conversion when they ask themselves, 'Why am I rich while there are so many poor around me?'"[20]

By viewing Romero's conversion as a realization, or awareness, of social sin, we can better account for that collective sense of it as historical sin or what the Bible calls the "sin of the world." Using the language of older moral theology, we can say that its value is that it posits a role for conversion that does not deny the existence of material sin (as the violation of God's will for the world) simply because there may not be formal sin (as evil done with freedom, intent, or knowledge).[21] With this understanding of social sin, we can understand the proper response of *conversio* not just as a turning away from personal sin but as a "seeing" of a larger, historical, social sin that demands participation in turning it back or removing it. To put it liturgically, conversion means a historical participation in the work of the Lamb of God who takes away the sin of the world.

---

19. See Kenneth R. Himes, "Social Sin and the Role of the Individual," *Annual of the Society of Christian Ethics* (1986): 183-218.

20. Oscar Romero, *La voz de los sin voz: La palabra viva de Monseñor Romero*, 2d ed. (San Salvador: UCA Editores, 1986), 317.

21. Ignacio Ellacuría draws attention to "historical sin" by noting that what goes down in history is not the intentionality of human acts (*opus operans*), but the objective result of acts (*opus operatum*). See Ignacio Ellacuría, "Church of the Poor," in *Ignacio Ellacuría: Essays on History, Liberation and Salvation,* ed. Michael E. Lee (Maryknoll, NY: Orbis Books, 2013).

Romero's conversion involves a "seeing anew," and I believe that that vision is a confrontation with the reality of social sin that demanded a response. Romero's response is best summed up as a preferential option for the poor, but as powerful a suggestion as this may be, even it can be easily ideologized. Romero's new way of "seeing" and responding can too easily become a paternalistic charity that empties any voice, any agency, from the other who is named "poor." This is not the *testimonio* of Romero. For Romero's new vision led him to exercise power in a different way. It led him to seek advice. It led him to the silence of contemplation before the stories of those who hungered and thirsted for justice, those who suffered persecution for the sake of the kingdom. It led him to start his homilies with their experiences and not his own. Romero's "seeing anew" led him to reconfigure his ministry in a way that recalibrated powerful social dynamics. No understanding of his conversion is complete without exploring that recalibration, one that reveals itself as a coming home.

Conversion and Returning Home

In perhaps Romero's most eloquent account of his transformation, he describes it to Cesar Jerez as a return home.

> It's just that we all have our roots, you know . . . I was born into a poor family. I've suffered hunger. I know what it's like to work from the time you're a little kid. . . . When I went to seminary and started my studies, and then they sent me to finish studying here in Rome, I spent years and years absorbed in my books, and I started to forget about where I came from. I started creating another world. When I went back to El Salvador, they made me the bishop's secretary in San Miguel. I was a parish priest for 23 years there, but I was still buried under paperwork. And when they sent me to San Salvador to be auxiliary bishop, I fell into the hands of Opus Dei, and there I remained. . . .
>
> Then they sent me to Santiago de María, and I ran into extreme poverty again. Those children that were dying just because of the water they were drinking, those campesinos killing themselves in the harvests. . . . You know, Father, when a piece of charcoal has already been lit once, you don't have to blow on it much to get it to flame up again. And everything that happened to us when I got to the archdiocese, what happened

to Father Grande and all . . . it was a lot. You know how much I admired him. When I saw Rutilio dead, I thought, "If they killed him for what he was doing, it's my job to go down that same road. . . ." So yes, I changed. But I also came back home again.[22]

Romero did have humble roots, and his return home is an odyssey from unreality back to a reality that he had forgotten or repressed. Yet, he did not return to his childhood. The "return home" actually served as an unsettling of the home into which he moved as he became archbishop and into a future that he could not anticipate. The image of a return home that is both hoped for but unsettling, then, draws out the implications of Romero's conversion.

Romero's image of home has elements of what postmodern and postcolonial thinkers have called the "unhomely." In Freud's thought, the *unheimliche* is, "that species of the frightening that goes back to what was once well-known and had long been familiar."[23] Though most often rendered "uncanny," the *unheimliche* is literally the "un-home-ly." As unhomely it is unsettling; it is a truth that a person must come to grips with even though they would wish to avoid it. This insight is given a political valence in Julia Kristeva's work *Strangers to Ourselves*, which indicates the way that recognizing how strange I am to myself helps me to recognize how the strangeness of the other is not a threat to my self-identity.[24] For Homi Bhabha, the "unhomely" serves the interruption of static identities and binaries that make up the colonial reality.[25] These are the kind of binaries at the heart of an expression like *haz patria, mata un cura* ("be a patriot, kill a priest"), the motto on leaflets distributed by right-wing death squads in El Salvador after the assassination of Rutilio Grande.

Theologically, this notion of the "unhomely" resonates with what Johannes Metz calls dangerous memories, those memories of the

---

22. As told to Cesar Jerez in López Vigil, *Memories*, 158-59.

23. Sigmund Freud, "The 'Uncanny,'" in *The Standard Edition of the Complete Psychological Works of Sigmund Freud, vol. XVII (1917-1919): An Infantile Neurosis and Other Works* (London: Hogarth Press, 1964), 220-26.

24. Julia Kristeva, *Strangers to Ourselves* (New York: Columbia University Press, 1991).

25. Homi Bhabha, *The Location of Culture* (New York: Routledge Press, 1994).

victims of history,[26] those memories that undercut the triumphal narratives of the victors and indicate the interconnectedness of all subjects. Romero's "return home" actually involves the "unhomely" interruption of his role as archbishop and sets his ministry on a new course.

Unhomeliness indicates how Romero did not become a "voice of the voiceless" who, reified in his position of power and independence, deploys his words in replacement or as an erasure of the voice of the poor. No, Romero becomes the "voice of the voiceless" by allowing those with no voice to speak their truth. Whether it was the interpersonal exchange with the multitude of *campesinos* lined up to speak to him (while leaving the Bishops' Conference), or the homilies in the cathedral whose news of the week recounted the sufferings and stories of this repressed population, Romero let the unhomely reality of the poor interrupt the flow of agency.

Romero's "return home" is not the departure from one "archbishop's" or "privileged" world and a return to a clearly specified *campesino* or "oppressed" world, but really the blurring of that which would conceive of them as two distinct worlds. Both Romero's personal history and the very nature of his office were rooted in colonial relationships of power that configured them historically. His conversion, then, lies more clearly in the "unhomely" existence that blurs the binary opposition, and, out of that blurring, creates a space for the archbishop to discover Oscar and for the church to be the *pueblo de Dios*. Romero's ecclesial motto, *Sentir con la iglesia* ("to think/feel with the church") is interruptive, as it blurs Romero's and the church's identities, and redirects them to incarnation and solidarity that makes manifest the reign of God.

As Ignacio Ellacuría put it,

> When the people represented hardly anything to [Romero], he hardly represented anything to the people, we used to say. Now we can add that when the people finally did become important to him, his announcement of the gospel finally had force; it was finally credible. It was not any force, but the evangelical force of salvation, the historical force of liberation.[27]

---

26. Johann Baptist Metz, *Faith in History and Society: Toward a Practical Fundamental Theology,* trans. and ed. J. Matthew Ashely (New York: Crossroad, 2007).

27. Ignacio Ellacuría, "Monseñor Romero: One Sent by God to Save His People," in Lee, *Ignacio Ellacuría,* 189.

Conclusion

I will conclude with an image. In her diary, Jean Donovan talks about the powerful experience of standing guard by the body of Archbishop Romero before his funeral. It is appropriate. For if the legacy of Romero is a conversion and incarnation in the world of the poor, then the guardians of that *testimonio* here in the United States are those like Jean Donovan, Ita Ford, Dorothy Kazel, and Maura Clarke. They witness not just against the more bellicose voices like Alexander Haig, Jeanne Kirkpatrick, and those who inherited their mantle, but those four women testify against the temptation to hide from the reality of the poor or rationalize it away. Finally, we can add the name of Dean Brackley, who in 1989 left my campus at Fordham University to go to San Salvador. It was a going away and a going home for Dean. After his death, a Mass on our campus was followed by a time of remembrances by those who worked in community organizing with Dean in the South Bronx. In their voices and their stories, Dean returned home again.

Romero's *testimonio* is one of conversion. It is prophecy. It is politics. It is wisdom. For me, Romero's conversion offers hope that we might have eyes to see and ears to hear. However, it is not the conversion of Romero the liberal hero, who single-handedly takes on the establishment; not a paternalistic Romero who saves a faceless poor through his largesse; not even an ecclesiastical Romero whose sanctity and fidelity are bleached of any real incarnation. No, his conversion is a journey of transformation that brought him to see all things anew in the face of social sin and led him home to the reality of a crucified people for whom, in a preferential option, he entrusted his office, his voice, and ultimately his destiny. His conversion embodies what Christians term *kenosis*, an outpouring of self that imitates the humble incarnation of God into the world. Hopefully, we can in our humble ways receive Romero's testimony and stand with Jean, Ita, Maura, Dorothy, Dean, and the other cloud of witnesses who have returned home.

13

The Jesuit Martyrs of 1989 and the Situation of the Church and World Today

Jon Sobrino, S.J.

I have a text here in Spanish. I will not read the text, and certainly not in Spanish.[1] I will try to speak freely in English. My English used to be fairly good. These days it is not that good. But hopefully I will make myself understood. "Why English?" you will say. It is best to speak the language that all of us have in common, and today, as we said, we remember something that is very important for many of us—certainly for me, and for you. So, in other words, today will not be the day for me to give a purely conceptual presentation.

I will talk from reality. The principle of reality is something that philosophers think about. In fact, I had the chance to get to know, live with, and work with Ignacio Ellacuría. For Ellacuría—one of the martyrs—concepts are very important. But they always come in second place, and for many in third place; and trying to develop concepts from other concepts is important. But maybe with us here today reality is very important. So I will talk from the reality that has been given to me as a Christian theologian. That is the first thing I want to say.

My second reflection has to do with the word "martyr." I will go into this word more conceptually as well. The word "martyr" is not just any type of word. At the very least it connotes two realities for me. One is blood. If there is no blood, there are no martyrs. Martyrs might

---

1. This essay is an edited transcription of the lecture delivered in English at DePaul University on November 16, 2013. The editors' emendations are found in square brackets.

be witnesses of something, but they are always blood, shed blood. So from a simple analysis of reality, "martyr" means or connotes two things: one is blood; there has been blood. And second, or first, if you wish, logically, it connotes love. Do you see love around this planet? I myself do not know. This is something for you to decide, whether you see love or not. In any case martyrs connote love.

Another thing I want to say, from the beginning, is that "martyr," although the word might sound a little bit exceptional—if you wish esoteric, some strange thing—it is not such an esoteric thing. In Latin America, and I imagine in other places, there have been many, many, many martyrs. Now who are they? Romero: yes, as Michael Lee has already shown so well. Romero is *fairly* well known. Do not think that he is *very* well known. Do not think that everybody in El Salvador today—certainly those who killed him—truly knew who he was. But they are not the only ones. Even among young seminarians, believe it or not, Romero is not very well known.

That means that to a certain degree or to a large degree, the church, or at least the Catholic Church, is going downward. But besides Romero, and as I said, Ellacuría, there have been thousands of peasants, some workers in the fields, also people like lawyers, students, teachers, and so on. And there have been, in El Salvador alone, sixteen or seventeen priests, members of the Catholic Church—I don't know if you know about that—who have been assassinated. There were also five sisters, one of them Salvadoran, and the other four, Irish nuns; and there were also two bishops: one, Archbishop Romero, and the other one, Bishop [Roberto Joaquín] Ramos. So martyrs are not something anecdotal; they are not an exception.

Going further into the simple analysis, the martyrs I have mentioned—the sixteen priests, the nuns, the bishops—look in life and death like Jesus of Nazareth. For me that is a very good thing to say because I think I have seen it, and I have come to that conclusion. But not any Jesus of Nazareth. From the beginning, I want to say something that maybe sounds a little bit scandalous: the Jesus of Luke. Why Luke, and not Mark and Matthew, or John? Because, according to Luke chapter 6, Jesus said [paraphrasing], "Blessed art thou, the poor, for you I have good news. You are hungry but you will eat; and you cry, but you will smile. But to all of you others: damned be you!" That Jesus of Nazareth according to Luke himself *was* and preached

good news for certain ones—the poor, the small ones—and bad news
for other people; the idea is not to insult people just for the sake of it,
or because it feels good or even that one may feel better or superior to
those insulted; that is not the reason. The issue is that Jesus of Nazareth had very, very hard and harsh words against certain people, and
that is why, by the way, Jesus himself became a martyr. He was killed.
You cannot go around saying those things and live long years and die
in bed surrounded by grandchildren.

Now we call, or I call, this type of people today who are killed
roughly, more or less, like Jesus—we call them "Jesuanic martyrs,"
mártires jesuanicos—so people who were very much like Jesus. They
are known and loved among our people. They belong to the tradition
of the Salvadoran church.

But now a second important subject, in my opinion, the most
important one, in fact. In Latin America there have been a larger
number of people who have been killed, far larger than the two arch-
bishops. There have been six or seven bishops in Latin America who
have been assassinated. None of them have been canonized, and I
return to this question below. And who are those people, larger in
number, than bishops or nuns? Well, they are poor people, those
who are below [i.e., at the margins of] history, who have been assassinated, often in large massacres. Those of you who are familiar with
El Salvador, at least you might remember El Mozote [December 10-11,
1981]—almost one thousand people—it is an awful number. Sumpul
is another massacre [May 14, 1980]. Sumpul is a river that divides Salvadoran land from Honduran land. And within El Salvador quite a
few peasants wanted to leave the place where they were because the
army, the official army, a death squad, followed them, and they found
themselves by the river. Some, I do not know how many, could swim,
and many others could not swim; and so the women and the children could not swim, but they tried to go across the river. Some of
them were drowned, and others were killed on the other side of the
river. And talking to someone today, the man was so nice to give me
a booklet on Acteal. Acteal is a place in Mexico where some years
ago there was another massacre [December 22, 1997]. By the way,
beyond Romero and Ellacuría, thousands of people in El Salvador,
and in Guatemala it is about the same or worse, because in Guatemala
it happened to the indigenous, and people despise them.

So who are these people? First of all, they are multitudes, a large number of people. In them, persons like Romero placed their hearts. That is why Bishop Romero, I think, appreciated us Jesuits at the university, but his heart was [primarily] among those hundreds of thousands of people. He had to hear very often the complaints of wives [and] mothers, whose husbands and children had been killed. But what I want to stress is that, for people like Romero and others, this large majority was at the center of their lives. My comment now, simple and brief, is that in their lives they [the poor] were oppressed, repressed, and massacred—not all of them, but many, many of them—and in death they are ignored. Romero is not ignored. As you hear from Monsignor Urioste—he was a very close friend of Romero; he says Romero was, and still is, the most loved, beloved Salvadoran, and the most hated Salvadoran. I think he is basically right.

Those peasants who died in massacres or of hunger did not have names. In death they are ignored. I cannot know—no one can know—how many millions of people have been assassinated on this planet. They are not the type of reality that we should study in some course at a university [but are subsequently forgotten]. And what happened? In El Salvador, Monsignor Romero and Ignacio Ellacuría gave them a name, and now they have a name. Maybe you have heard it among you. Ellacuría and Romero, in this situation, called them "the crucified people." That is important—for me it is very important: now they have a name! They are not those who do not exist, the crucified people. It is important because *people* means not only more than one, but more than a dozen, and more than a thousand, means a large majority; and *crucified*, of course, is metaphorical language—they get crucified with nails and a cross, but it is a metaphor that conveys reality. These people get killed, innocently, unjustly, as Jesus was; and the word *crucified*, also on the lips of a priest like Ellacuría, who was also a philosopher, and of a bishop like Romero, conveys the idea that this is a Christian community. Likewise, both of them also call those large majorities the "Suffering Servant of Yahweh." Men and women were killed like Romero—in fact more men than women, but also women—because they defended the crucified people. Conceptually this may not sound very deep, but we are going beyond language of the heart [in order] to think through things.

Why was Jesus of Nazareth killed? Why did he die on a cross? Now, of course, there is an answer that is true, but it is not the total truth: it was the will of the Father. Okay. Why was it the will of the Father? Who knows? At least, I do not know. But why did Jesus of Nazareth, a good man, a just man, end up at the cross? Was it that he made the option for the poor? Yes. Did he make only the option for the poor? No.

But if you read what the bishops at Puebla said, they said that independently of [the] moral situation [of the poor], or their personal situation, God, what God does is going to be gratuitous. And what does God do gratuitously? Two things: the first one [is that] "God defends [the poor] and loves them"—defends them, so [God] actively, actively, goes out of himself to defend them.

Why do you have to defend someone? Defend from what? And [thus] the bishops at Pueblo said, "God defends them and loves them." Now this is the option for the poor. What happens [is that] some people understand [that] we have to make the option for the poor, we have to love the poor, help the poor—really!—by the very fact that they are poor; but we might help the poor without having to fight against anyone. If poverty is only material scarcity and no one is responsible for that . . . [but] defending the poor means that you have to be against [those] who attack the poor. As for those who defend the poor and confront enemies who attack them, they are persecuted, defamed, insulted, and killed. And, by the way, that is the ABCs of the gospel narrative. Jesus was not killed because he was—I'm serious—a nice man, because he was too kind to the poor, or even merciful and understanding with sinners; that he was, and that is very important, and we all try and imitate that. But Jesus was killed because, beyond that, he confronted the Pharisees (however one understands that sect's historical reality), the Sadducees, the scribes, the wealthy, and certainly the high priests, that is, those who had real power.

So what am I trying to say? When we talk about martyrs, when we talk about the people, when we talk about those thousands of people, they are also the cause, the reason, why individual people, the Jesuanic martyrs, get killed, when they try to defend them. Archbishop Romero, the day before he was killed said, "In the name of God" (Romero really talked about God) "and in the name of these suffering people whose cries reached to heaven." And then he talked to the soldiers and said, "Brothers, you belong to the same people, and in the name of God you can't do that. So in the name of God I ask you,

I beg you, I order you, I command you: stop the repression!" So did Romero help the poor? Obviously? Was he nice to the poor? Indeed. But he went beyond. He confronted those who were the enemies of the poor. And that's why the Jesuanic martyrs are identified as such, because they have defended the crucified people.

Now the point is that in our world today (not just in El Salvador with peasants, massacres), with or without globalization, with or without the celebration of the end to global poverty (I think the rate of poverty should have decreased 50 percent; that was said ten years ago), with or without the World Youth Days—in all that, in the world I have described a little bit ironically, millions of human beings continue suffering, unjustly and innocently, [suffering] violent deaths in repression, wars, and massacres. And many more millions suffer slow death. That is why I began with the two ideas, blood and love, where blood is the symbol of death. Millions suffer slow death because of poverty. The more we know about the world situation, the more [we need to listen to] people like Hans Ziegler, a professor at the University of Geneva in Switzerland before being commissioned by the United Nations as Special Rapporteur on the Right to Food. He writes that children do not die out of hunger. They are assassinated. And he stressed—he is correct, and it is the point—*assassinated*, because today the world can solve the problem of at least minimal nourishment.

Pedro Casaldáliga, from Brazil, born in Catalonia, Spain, wrote rather recently:

> Today there is more wealth on earth, but there is also more injustice. 1.5 billion people survive on earth with less than two Euros a day, and 25,000 people die every day of hunger according to the Food and Agriculture Organization of the United Nations. Desertification threatens the life of 1.2 billion people in one hundred countries. The migrants are denied their fraternity, the ground under their feet. The United States builds a wall of 1,500 kilometers against Latin America. In Europe, southern Spain builds a fence against Africa. All this is wicked, but intentional.[2]

---

2. Pedro Casaldáliga, "Utopia es necesaria como el pan de cada día," *El País*, January 30, 2006, http://firgoa.usc.es/drupal/node/25478.

Well I do not know whether Casaldáliga has the exact figures or not, but this is our world. These are the crucified people. And just since I come from El Salvador, in El Salvador, in twelve years of war, 75,000 people were assassinated from both sides so to speak, although it has been figured out that of the total, maybe 4 percent were killed by the guerilla movement, and the rest by government and by death squads. But that was it. The war was over, and people do not hear about El Salvador anymore, right? I may be wrong. It does not exist, El Salvador. As I said before, the crucified people do not even have a name. Ignacio Ellacuría called them by name, "crucified people."

In the last twenty years since the peace accord in 1992, so roughly twenty years, 100,000 people have been assassinated. There are many things to say about it. The first one is the fact. And do not think I am just exaggerating. Why? Well, there are many, many problems, gangs, and a drug trade. So it is complicated. I think at the very end it all ends up with those who accumulate lots of wealth—but anyway, whatever the last reason is, [they are] the crucified people in El Salvador.

[Now we may turn to a] conceptual distinction, because concepts work for people who are aware of theology! It used to be said in general in the theology books, when the theme of martyrdom came up, that martyrs were those who were killed out of *odium fidei* [hatred of the faith], which means those who killed [did so] because they hated the Christian religion or Catholic religion, to put it simply. Now, of course, what I have described—in El Salvador, as far as I know—nobody has been killed, not even Romero (who really believed in God and prayed to God and said wonderful things about God)—was killed in *odium fidei*. He was killed, like Ellacuría, in *odium iustitiae* [hatred of justice]. There are things that other people cannot stand. Why is it? It might be original sin, which is to say something that means a lot and might mean nothing, but anyway, that is the way we human beings are. They killed them not because of the hatred of faith, but rather because of the hatred of justice.

Now Karl Rahner, when he was seventy-nine, the year before he died, he was asked to write an article in the journal called *Concilium*[3] on martyrdom, and he wrote [the] four pages right away, and he said,

---

3. Karl Rahner, "Dimensions of Martyrdom: A Plea for the Broadening of a Classical Concept," *Concilium* 163.3 (1983): 9-11.

confronting this problem of *in odium fide/in odium iustitiae*, "Why should Monsignor Romero not be a martyr? He fell in the struggle for justice, in a struggle that he made based on his most profound Christian convictions."

So Karl Rahner was saying—the old Karl Rahner, not a young liberation theologian or something like that, but he was a man with *sensus fidei*, and he said in my own words, "You tell me that Romero is not a martyr? What type of frame do we have? What type of theology have we built, in which Romero cannot be a martyr?" And he showed [this], again in the same article, speaking about Maximilian Kolbe. So Rahner commented that Pope [Paul VI] canonized Maximilian Kolbe, not as martyr, but as confessor—for the distinction between martyr and confessor was in order. So what do I want to say? That people gave up their own lives out of love so that they are killed—apparently that is not good [enough] to be a martyr, ([while], of course, you have to be very "intelligent," or at least a little bit, to read in the Gospel of John that no one has a greater love than he or she who gives his life away [John 15:13]).

So all I want to stress, talking today about the six Jesuits and the two women, the issue of who they were. [They were] members of the crucified people. As I said and insist upon, Romero and Ellacuría gave them a name—of course a general name, because they did not know the names of the thousands of people who have been killed. They are the "crucified people."

Another conceptual distinction that needs to be made is that the word "martyr" in English comes from the Greek *martys*, which means "witness." Now I have to raise the question (without trying to be conceptual): "Are martyrs witnesses?" Yes, martyrs give a witness of love. Are they only witnesses? No, they are more than that. What are they? Sacraments. What am I trying to say? This is for you, and for you theologians to comment on. Martyrs are not only those who with their death give evidence of Jesus. [They] are the sacraments who make Jesus present. And, thinking of that, I come back to something Ellacuría said three days before Romero was assassinated at the university where they had a Mass; and Ellacuría at one moment, he said, "With Monsignor Romero, God walked through (*Dios pasó por*) El Salvador." Is that giving witness? Yes, but it is more: [he] made God present. A theological word for that would be "sacrament," but that's not very important, I think.

To go from *odium fidei* to *odium iustitiae* was a substantial advance. In theology that had not been the case. A martyr was somebody who was killed in *odium fidei*. But to say a martyr who was killed can be and is somebody who was killed in *odium iustitiae* was a great step forward. But, in my opinion, it is not yet the most fundamental advancement. From a *theologal* perspective ("theologal" means from the perspective of God), this development consists, in my opinion, in *naming*, and naming with names that connote dignity.

The crucified people were given titles of dignity. And they were called the "crucified people" and "the Suffering Servant of Yahweh." Remember in Isaiah, the four songs of the servant of Yahweh (42:1-4; 49:1-6; 50:4-11; 52:13-53:12). The fourth one [depicts] the Suffering Servant, [and] the servant of Yahweh is suffering still. Ellacuría also said that the "crucified people" is the servant of God. Romero used to prepare his homilies reading good and normal biblical traditions for the readings, and when he came to this reading of the Suffering Servant, he said, "How fitting it is that the biblical scholars don't agree; some think one way; some think [another] way. Some think that the Suffering Servant of Yahweh, who was not a real historical figure, might mean the whole people, or the future Jesus Christ." The nice thing about Romero's comment, [while] he did not solve the biblical problem or give his opinion, is that with the same word we can think of Jesus of Nazareth who will be our savior or [think of] the people.

What I am trying to say, quoting Ellacuría, and for Romero, is that the Suffering Servant of Yahweh was the people, the little people, the ten thousands. How is the Suffering Servant of Yahweh described in Isaiah? In chapters 52 and 53, some things that the prophet Isaiah—or whoever the prophet may be, Second Isaiah—found in that Suffering Servant [were that] the Suffering Servant (the crucified people) is a man of sorrows, acquainted with grief. He is despised, disfigured, no longer looks like a human being, and many are horrified by him (52:14; 53:3). Here is my comment: today, the tortures have left them. When you see the crucified people, they produce horror and disgust; many are frightened by [this Suffering Servant] (52:14). Before him they hide their faces (53:3). It is a disgusting [thing] to see them. [We hope] that they may not perturb the happiness of the world of abundance.

Suffering, poor, disdained, disregarded, insulted, denied even their own religiosity, the peasants in El Salvador were called "communist." (And some of them were.) The peasants did not even know who Karl Marx was. But to call somebody a communist was to insult somebody.

Now [here is] my general comment: all [this] is carried in their own flesh, today; [with] the "crucified people." Isaiah says the following about the servant today: "They bury him among the wicked" (53:9). In fact, [the crucified people are] missing, as the bodies [were] dumped in landfills in clandestine cemeteries; they had had no grave and no epitaph. They have not been buried among sinners, which is awful. We do not even know where they have been buried.

Concerning the servant, Isaiah says, "He did not open his mouth, like a lamb led to the slaughter" (53:7). Today we do have groups that defend [the poor], such as human rights organizations. But the vast majority of the crucified people do not open their mouths—most of them because they are already dead, or they are relatives and are really scared. [Again,] of the servant, Isaiah says, "They took him; without defense, they will have justice" (53:8). Today it has also occurred—the massacres in total helplessness and powerlessness. Of the servant, Isaiah says that he is innocent: "there was no deceit in his mouth, nor had he committed any crime" (53:9).

So that is Isaiah; what I am trying to say is that when Romero and Ellacuría used this expression, "the crucified people, the Suffering Servant of Yahweh," they were not naïve. They knew of the problems and sins of the crucified people; but in general, put together, compared to their executioners, that is what they say about the crucified people. And I think this is true to the present [day]. And I ask myself rhetorically, "What sin have the indigenous of Guatemala, who were burned within the church of San Francisco in Huehuetenango, committed? What about the peasants killed in El Mozote? What about the children who have died of starvation in Africa? What have they done?"

Well, in summary that is what I wanted to say. Today, November 16, we remember the Salvadoran martyrs. Some of them are well known: Ellacuría, Ignacio Martín-Baró (because he studied here). But, anyway, I have wanted to add another type of [category]—I do not call them martyrs anymore, Jesuanic martyrs—[so that there] not be a confusion with language—but I call them, or we call them, "crucified people, the Suffering Servant of Yahweh."

And [moving on] to the end, my last reflection is the following. El Salvador: it is a wonderful country, it is a terrible country—it is a place of human beings; that is more important than being wonderful. Once John the Baptist was to be jailed, Jesus of Nazareth started to emerge. So John the Baptist [was] in jail, while he was not yet a martyr—later he was beheaded—but the[re] was a succession, if you like. [While] John the Baptist was in jail, I do not know why Jesus says, "Now is my time." (It was existential. It is psychology. It makes sense to say this.) [In] El Salvador Rutilio Grande was assassinated [on] March 12, 1977; that very night Archbishop Romero emerged. March 24, 1980. I will quote what [a] woman told me, "[When] Monsignor was assassinated, [then] Ignacio Ellacuría emerged." That was one way of looking for parallelisms. Somebody was killed—some [great] one, so another one emerged. So I think—I say this in all simplicity—El Salvador has been a country in which it has not been so easy to kill the martyrs for good. Because another one [always] emerges.

What do we do now? My last reflection [concerns when] I was in Thailand [at the time] when the Jesuits were killed. From Thailand I flew to San Francisco and then to Santa Clara University, and I started writing. And I did not write to publish or to publish an article on the martyrs. No, I wanted to talk to myself. I did not know how to end [it]. [So] I did with this quote, with these words: "May they rest in peace, Ignacio Ellacuría, Ignacio Martín-Baró, Segundo Montes, Joaquín López (y López), Juan Moreno, and Armando López: may they rest in peace, brothers and fellow journeyers with Jesus; may Celina and Elba Ramos also rest in peace, daughters truly loved by God. May they rest in peace; may they never allow us to rest in peace."

Contributors

J. Matthew Ashley is Associate Professor and Chair of the Department of Theology at the University of Notre Dame. In 1998 he wrote *Interruptions: Mysticism, Politics and Theology in the Work of Johann Baptist Metz,* and he has recently coedited (with Kevin Burke, S.J., and Rodolfo Cardenal, S.J.) *A Grammar of Justice: The Legacy of Ignacio Ellacuría* (2014).

Agnes Brazal is Professor, Graduate Program Coordinator, and Director of the Office for Research and Publications at the St. Vincent School of Theology at Adamson University in Manila, Philippines. Her forthcoming book (with Emmanuel S. de Guzman) is entitled *Intercultural Church: Bridge of Solidarity in the Migration Context.*

Maria Clara Bingemer is Associate Professor of Theology at the Pontifical Catholic University of Rio de Janeiro. In 2010, 2012, and 2014, she was a Visiting Research Fellow at DePaul University's Center for World Catholicism and Intercultural Theology. Her works in English include (with Ivone Gebara) *Mary: Mother of God, Mother of the Poor* (1989). Her latest book, *O mistério e o mundo. Paixão por Deus em tempos de descrença* (2013), will soon appear in English translation.

Michael Budde is Professor and Chair of the Department of Catholic Studies, Professor (and former chair) of Political Science, and Senior Research Fellow in the Center for World Catholicism and Intercultural Theology at DePaul University. His most recent book is entitled *The Borders of Baptism: Identities, Allegiances and the Church* (2011).

Peter Casarella is Associate Professor of Theology at the University of Notre Dame. He served until 2013 as founding Director of the Center for World Catholicism and Intercultural Theology at DePaul University and coedited with Raúl Gómez *Cuerpo de Cristo: The Hispanic Presence in the U.S. Catholic Church* (1998).

William T. Cavanaugh is Director of the Center for World Catholicism and Intercultural Theology at DePaul University. His books include *Torture and Eucharist: Theology, Politics, and the Body of Christ* (1998), *The Myth of Religious Violence: Secular Ideology and the Roots of Modern Conflict* (2009), and *Migrations of the Holy: Theologies of State and Church* (2011).

Paulo Carneiro Fernando de Andrade is the Dean of the Center of Theology and Human Sciences at the Pontifical Catholic University of Rio de Janeiro. He is also a past president of SOTER (Brazilian Society of Theology and Religious Studies), one of the founders of the World Forum for Theology and Liberation, and a former vice-president of INSeCT (International Network of Societies for Catholic Theology).

Michael E. Lee is Associate Professor in the Department of Theology at Fordham University and is President of the Academy of Catholic Hispanic Theologians in the U.S. for 2013-2014. He has published *Bearing the Weight of Salvation: The Soteriology of Ignacio Ellacuría* (2009), and recently edited *Ignacio Ellacuría: Essays on History, Liberation, and Salvation* (2013).

João Batista Libânio, S.J., was formerly of the Jesuit Faculty of Philosophy and Theology in Belo Horizonte, Brazil. He went to the Lord on January 30, 2014, after dedicating his life to the promotion of the theology of liberation in Brazil.

Juan Carlos Scannone, S.J., is Professor of Theology at the Universidad del Salvador in San Miguel, Argentina. He collaborated in developing the Argentine school of "Theology of the People" and is currently a writer-in-residence at *La civiltà cattolica*, an Italian cultural journal of the Society of Jesus.

Jon Sobrino, S.J., is Professor of Theology and Member of the Board of Directors at the University of Central America in San Salvador, El Salvador. He is also the Director of the Monseñor Romero Center at the Universidad Centroamericana and the co-director of the journal *Revista latinoamericana de teología*. His many books include *Witnesses to the Kingdom: The Martyrs of El Salvador and the Crucified Peoples* (2003), *Where Is God? Earthquake, Terrorism, Barbarity, and*

Hope (2004), *No Salvation outside the Poor: Prophetic-Utopian Essays* (2008). With Ignacio Ellacuría he edited *Mysterium Liberationis: Fundamental Concepts of Liberation Theology* (1993).

Andrew Prevot is Assistant Professor of Theology at Boston College. He completed his doctorate in 2013 at the University of Notre Dame with a dissertation entitled "Thinking Prayer: Doxology, Spirituality, and the Crises of Modernity."

Todd Walatka serves as the Assistant Chair for Graduate Studies in Theology at the University of Notre Dame. He completed his Ph.D. at Notre Dame in 2011 with a dissertation that engaged the work of Hans Urs von Balthasar through the lens of Jon Sobrino and Latin American liberation theology.

Index